THE CHURCH,
PILGRIM OF CENTURIES

The Church, Pilgrim of Centuries

THOMAS MOLNAR

William B. Eerdmans Publishing Company
Grand Rapids, Michigan

Copyright © 1990 by Wm. B. Eerdmans Publishing Co.
255 Jefferson Ave. S.E., Grand Rapids, Mich. 49503

Printed in the United States of America

Library of Congress Cataloging-in-Publication Data

Molnar, Thomas Steven.
　　The church, pilgrim of centuries / Thomas Molnar.
　　　　p.　　　cm.
　　ISBN 0-8028-0420-9
　　1. Catholic Church—History—1965-　I. Title.
BX1390.M65　1990
282′.09′045—dc20　　　　　　　　　　　90-41597
　　　　　　　　　　　　　　　　　　　　　　　　CIP

Contents

Introduction

It is risky to write about an ongoing series of events, in this case the Catholic church's history in the second half of the twentieth century. Risky because since the Second Vatican Council the church's stability has been put in question; in fact it has been said by some that it is undergoing a revolution in the manner of the great revolutions of our time. But while the latter toppled kings, desacralized ancient institutions, and replaced traditional beliefs with new dogmas, such things did not happen in the church. It is therefore said by others that the Vatican Council merely instituted reforms somewhat difficult for various groups of believers to accept: all will quiet down in the end; the church will continue to minister to the faithful, and will coexist in peace with society.

As we, listening to signs of the next millennium, try to understand the events in and around the church, a certain number of realities shape our diagnosis. Most of them will be discussed in the pages of this book. Here I will mention only a few in order to provide a framework within which events best can be grasped.

Today, a quarter of a century after the end of Vatican II, the church is seen as battered, not unlike some ex-great powers (I have France and England in mind) which, although on the victorious side of the war, are now exhausted, without their former energy, self-assurance, and the dynamism of expansion. If we still speak of them as "great powers," it is by habit of language and in memory of past greatness. Some remnants of prestige still linger on, but they are like empty shells: the content has been drained.

Now the church appears to us in the same light. The war it fought had its central battlefield in the conciliar chamber and in the offices where the documents were planned, elaborated, submitted for a vote, returned, modified, and accepted with the approval of the episcopal majority and of the Pope. However, many skirmishes also broke out on the side; in Rome and elsewhere a war raged far and wide, as always happens when man's philosophical foundations are debated. Thus what followed 1965 was not peace after a healthy and cleansing storm, but a landscape of devastation. The official church pretended that nothing happened, that in fact the turmoil was a positive thing. But mostly the indifferent ones believed this version of the events; those concerned, for or against, knew better: a "great power," a divinely guided and history-making institution, began to show signs of spiritual exhaustion. As in the case of England and France, the respectful words and gestures which still greeted the church's worldwide role even after Vatican II were due not to its sacredness and authority but to its past glory and achievements, the unity of its faith, the preaching of Jesus Christ, and the worldly splendor which accompanied and expressed its uniqueness.

Thus, in spite of the heavy layers of embellishing talk in and around the Roman institution, everybody during the last twenty-five years has been aware of the tensions, the loss of authority, the concessions, the weaknesses, and the disobedience within the church. It has become like a suddenly impoverished noble family, hardly able to keep up appearances, compelled to sell its furniture, marry off its children below its social level, and let people see the domestic quarrels and infidelities, the whole threadbare fabric.

What does such a family do? It works out a plan: counting the money, the jewelry, the bondpapers hidden in drawers; adopting practices below its dignity; contracting unwanted alliances with the powerful and the nouveaux riches. Consider one example: the ideology of man-centeredness which inspires and shapes our age, whether in its liberal or Marxist expression, has compelled the church after the Council to allow, although not yet to decree, communion in hand at what used to be the altar rail. Why this practice, why this insistence? Because the allies of the church's so-called progressive forces, the avant-garde, demand a series of measures or at least tolerated practices which then slowly become policy, as indications that not God but man is at the center of the new world and the post-conciliar church. This new master, man, wants to stand up from his kneeling posture, face God as an equal, and, symbolically, take or leave Christ's body. Every human act which is not the ordinary, day-to-day routine has the value of a symbol. Thus it is eminently significant that today the church's traditional symbols are not only watered down and declared expendable (and this includes sacraments in many dioceses and parishes); they are exchanged for another set of symbols meant to demonstrate man's maturity, adulthood, mastery.

Our illustration was only one among many; we could have chosen others because all arise from the same inspiration: man in the place of the Absolute. What naturally follows from it is society's general desacralization (announced already by Max Weber a hundred years ago, then by many other thinkers), and the sacralization of man, his rights, his ideologies, his lifestyles, his sexual choices. Very few speak about these things openly in ecclesiastical circles. It is not yet done—the "October Revolution of the Church" (theologian Yves Congar's expression for Vatican II) is still too close. But everyone knows that these things exist and have begun to prevail.

Some are lucid enough to know that the same things will continue because gestures, acts, words, and symbols are not empty—they have their logic and attract other similar gestures and words. We begin with communion in the hand, continue with sloppy and disrespectful clothing and behavior at Mass, and end with defiance of doctrine, morals, and the magisterium.

The series of events, the revolutionary changes, the losses and concessions with which we began this introduction are not suddenly going to stop, arbitrarily. Their continuation suggests, to be sure, further weaknesses and hesitations—but also changes in the other direction, slow because of the accumulated inertia, yet increasingly self-assertive. Twenty-five years is almost a generation, and the church counts in centuries. From 1965 (and even before) until 1990 the conciliar revolution expended so much of its energy and misguided enthusiasm—its adepts have so openly and completely showed their cards and revealed their ambitions—that in the end they have remained without arguments and ammunition. Had they presented sober reflections or conquered decisive institutional positions, they would not need now to camouflage their intentions, to play with loaded dice, to set fires which are spectacular but quick to die.

In short, the renewalists and rebels have opened themselves to counteractions and countermeasures. Indeed, when they throw all prudence and tact to the wind and demand the end of priestly celibacy, the ordination of women, sexual freedom, the liquidation of "patriarchalism" and "sexism," and women popes (as female theologians Uta Ranke-Heinemann in Germany and Rosemary Ruether in the United States do), what can they expect in following the mindless tactics of earlier heretics? What they did not expect has been a firmer and accelerated countermovement underway in Rome, a gradual dismantling of their absurd position, and finally a lonely stand from which to launch rage-filled verbal bombs that do no harm.

In other words, what has happened in the last twenty-five years—outside the public arena filled by media-noise, but in the minds and souls of believers and hierarchs, and simply in the innermost workings of providence—is a partial transformation from an alarmed, vacillating, ready-for-concessions mentality to a siege mentality in defense of positions which cannot be surrendered. And as soon as the besiegers show signs of weakness here and there, or impatience and brutality, the besieged issue forth, achieving small and local but significant victories.

Thus it is not unrealistic to forecast for the next twenty-five or fifty years a process of slow restoration to some sort of equilibrium. Optimism is not in order, for we do not even know whether we have reached the low point of this revolution. It seems, however, that faith and orthodoxy possess a resilience that utopia-fuelled radicalism lacks. It also seems that sacred history obstinately accompanies profane history, and comes to its rescue. What happened in Eastern Europe around Christmas 1989 was an anticipated Easter, a resurrection. Political developments are one thing, signs from God are another, but the two may work together for peace and the conversion of hearts.

CHAPTER ONE

The View from the Open Window

In 1961, a year before Pope John XXIII called together the Second Vatican Council (1962-65), an American company offered Catholic church officials a comparative efficiency study of the Vatican and General Electric. The proposal took for granted that here were two vast bureaucratic organizations—one of them never yet tested by modern methods—whose dynamism, in very different sectors of life, of course, were very nearly equal or at least similar to one another. It is not known whether the research company launched its project for self-publicity; the fact is, surprisingly, that the Vatican accepted the challenge. If memory serves me right, the verdict after several months of scrutiny was that both "enterprises" reached the highest standards in about equal measure.

That year, 1961, thus marked the semiofficial entry of the Roman church into the modern liberal-industrial world from which it had kept its distance throughout modern times, at least up until the end of the pontificate of Pius XII (1958). We now have the record of three decades, enabling us to assess the significance and the consequences of the *aggiornamento*, the "updating" or the "opening of the Vatican's windows to let in the fresh air of modernity." Thirty years are not perhaps enough to reach definitive judgments about matters as weighty as a new phase in the history of the institutional church. It is even more difficult to take this period—any period—of this institution's ongoing history, and, by focusing on that short moment, make it seem a decisive, indeed a culminating point. But the

1

questions asked—by both Catholics and others—ever since
the Council ended, have been of such import and urgency that
a balance sheet may be legitimately drawn up.

(*a*) Is the Roman Catholic process of *adaptation* to the
modern world a new form of apostolate, an attempt to formulate ways of approach to modern requirements and values; or

(*b*) is it a liquidation of the pre-conciliar church, amount-
ing to a *revolution,* as the influential Father Yves Congar called
it, directed against the traditional forms of institution and
authority?

The answers to these questions must be very prudent
indeed, in view of the extreme interpretations that have stolen
the limelight in the debate about the Council's significance.
One interpretation may be described as the *apocalyptic* view
that concludes with a despairing finality that this century will
witness the end of the church; the other is the *utopian* belief
that the real history of the church begins only now—that is,
with the Council, the new consciousness it has created, the
new religious quests and attitudes.

In view of such alarmed questions and hasty replies, we
must try to establish a reasonably accurate picture of the
church's place in our century. Such a description should
consider, first, the nature of the reality to which the church
now "opens its windows." What strikes the observer is the new
place that the church occupies vis-à-vis the state and civil
society, as well as among other institutions. From the vantage
point of the past, the separation of church and state was
certainly a momentous event; of equal importance is the reduced role of the church from being the traditional spiritual
guide of national communities and of larger *ensembles* (see the
medieval *christiana respublica*), to the status of an interest
group within civil society. Whether or not this development
was a historical necessity and as such positive or negative, it
does represent a new phase in the church's existence. It is also
a weighty phenomenon because it is the first time in the history
of mankind that religious authority (often referred to as
"Temple") is clearly separated from political authority (also
called "Palace" in the pertinent literature). This book is not a

history book; it does not deal with the fascinating chronicle of the relationship of spiritual and temporal powers, of the sacred and the profane.[1] The separation of church and state in constitutional and civil law that citizens in our century take for granted is, however, one of the major events of modern times that should not be judged on a doctrinaire basis but in terms of its observable consequences.

Many argue that this historic separation was a positive thing for the church (and religion in general) because it has removed the burden of the "altar serving the throne," and the church's political involvement with, and subservience to, the powerful. Those who argue in this manner tend to forget that the *locus* of power is not necessarily the state or the wealthy, as we have come to believe, but that power can also reside elsewhere: in pressure groups, democratically organized parties and labor unions, concentrations of business interests, ideologically inspired associations, the media, the culture heroes of the moment with their enthusiastic mass followers. At any rate, due to its recent separation from the state—its longtime "natural ally" in enforcing within community or nation a certain moral code and social discipline—the church fell from a position of central influence into a modest corner of pluralistic society, destined to become one interest group competing among the many.[2]

For now, some say, the gains balance the losses; the church may, for the first time since Emperor Constantine associated it to his power (A.D. 313), measure its own undiluted worth, since it is now judged on its own moral merits. Moreover, so the argument runs, the church can now enter alliances it used to

---

1. For this, see Thomas Molnar, *Twin Powers: Politics and the Sacred* (Grand Rapids: Eerdmans, 1988).

2. For a contrast with the modern situation, consider the views of the Abbot Suger, royal advisor and builder of churches in eleventh-century France. "Suger wanted to strengthen the power of the Crown of France, and to aggrandize the Abbey of St. Denis. To Suger these ambitions did not conflict with each other. They appeared to him as aspects of but one ideal which he believed to correspond both to natural law and to Divine Will . . . and their interests with those of the nation." Introduction to Ervin Panofsky, *Abbot Suger* (Princeton: Princeton University Press, 1979), p. 2.

spurn, fight for international causes, take the side of the weak, the poor, and the marginal against the power of the state and the privileged. Naturally, these implicit accusations against past historical forms ought to be examined with care, since the church has always focused much of its attention on the sick, the slave, the poor, the orphan.[3] The fact remains, however, that, measured in a general way, the church has lost much of the dynamism and authority that had shaped civilization and the ethical imagination for centuries, influencing marriage and family life, education, law, institutions, art and architecture, and, last but not least, the public debate.[4] Besides, the question arises and will occupy us in these pages whether separation from the state has not led the church to a new dependence on other power concentrations and social forces.

It would be naive to assume—as utopian mentalities tend to do—that with the democratic redistribution of power in the modern Western world the old nature has been thrown out and a new one ushered in. What is more probable is that the power relationships have changed: there are new ruling strata, new cults, newly advantaged segments of the population. At the same time there are new losers, new taboos, new censors, and also new voiceless categories, such as the eternal poor in spirit whom Jesus promised would always be with us.

Within a half century or so, tremendous transformations have taken place in the public landscape. The hierarchically articulated Western society—with state, church, and the constituted orders on top wielding from above a great influence through power, tradition, and imitation—has become a faded

3. My observations in the so-called underdeveloped parts of the world are that Christianity alone provides charitable institutions and social services to those in need, and runs orphanages, homes for handicapped children, old-age homes, trade schools for the poor, homes for unwed mothers, and of course hospitals. Moslems, Buddhists, Hindus, etc., whose religious faith cannot be doubted, are deficient in the creation of a charitable social network for the help of fellowmen.

4. It took the church two centuries (11th to 13th) to compel feudal society through a new legislation to regard concubinage as sinful and to accept marriage, elevated to a sacrament, as the only lawful and moral way of securing inheritance and rights of legitimate heirs.

memory known by a collection of yellowing photographs in an old album. Its place has been taken by an industrially near-equalized society, informed by a mixture of liberalism, socialism, and the cult of science and technology. The upper classes have been replaced by ubiquitous bureaucracies that are supposed to channel the new and amorphous masses as effectively as the nobility and clergy used to keep order among the old classes—more effectively, we are told, since the authority of the upper classes was founded on obedience, coercion, and reverence (sociologist Seymour Lipset still called British society a quarter of a century ago "reverential"), whereas the leadership of bureaucracies rests on acceptance and reasoned assent.

From the church's perspective, two important things have happened "out there" in the world as results of these epochal transformations. First, the state underwent changes, partly because of its separation from the church, partly because of society's new demands. Briefly, it has become the only visible "high authority" directing citizens' lives, passing laws, assuming new functions. To the state have come requests for decisions on all matters, from monetary policy to the organization of international sports events or withdrawal from them, as in the 1980 Moscow Olympic games. To be sure, the top officials of the state no longer wear military uniforms as a blatant sign of power, and they are no longer called kings, princes, and marshals; they are now presidents, ministers, general secretaries, and committee chairmen, and wear business suits and ties. The state, nevertheless, assumes the role of a "church," or at least adheres to an ideology which for all intents and purposes has become a substitute religion, not only in totalitarian, but also in democratic regimes.

One of the services the church traditionally rendered to the state was its role as spokesman for wide sectors of society. While shaping culture and the emotional world of citizens the church interpreted the public feelings and attitudes that civil authority had to take into account. However, through the historic separation the state has found itself obliged to become all things to all citizens: teacher, guide, protector, administrator, and organizer of collective existence. Whether in liberal or socialist regimes, the state is regarded in this century as the source of well-being, social justice, and a provider for every sectorial interest. No wonder that Italian liberal scholar Guido Ruggiero wrote as early as 1927 that liberals have finally become reconciled with the state they used to fear and execrate, because their agenda is now fulfilled by their former adversary.[5]

The modern, industrially-centered state, whether of the liberal or the welfare variety, has thus become a quasi-church, formulating its own belief system or adopting one defined by particularly strong pressure groups. Even in the United States, where, of all Western nations, *separation* was for the first time integrated into the Constitution, we speak of "secular humanism" as a belief system practically enforced by federal and state governments through such channels as court decisions, public agencies, education textbooks, universities, and the media. It is the "public philosophy," to use Walter Lippmann's expression. Facing this parallel religion, parallel to that of the mainline churches and elusive because it declines formulation and overt institutional manifestations, the Catholic church cannot hope to dispute the quasi-monopolistic position of the secular belief system. The church is free to live and be active in the milieu subtly determined by secular humanism, but it is at a distinct disadvantage—with its dogmas and moral code—in comparison to the built-in choice of citizens in a secular, liberal, and industrial society.

The second thing that happened, from the church's per-

---

5. Since we speak in these pages of the church in a generally Western, in parts planetary, context, we do not give the term *liberalism* its specific American connotation ("left of center"), but the worldwide meaning: free market, capitalist economy, individualism, the "nightwatchman state," rationalism in ultimate questions. By *socialism* we do not mean the Marxist variety (this will be referred to as communism) but the "tamed" kind, compatible with the beliefs and methods of liberal society. This socialism, even when it governs, subscribes to a mixed economy, the democratic alternation of parties in power, pluralism in culture, etc. The difference, in the discourse and program, is that socialists defend the "working class," impose high taxes on business, and preach a utopian future for mankind.

spective, is the extraordinary ascendence of civil society in the last two centuries. Civil society was a steadily growing rival of the state since the latter part of the Middle Ages and the foremost inspirer and organizer of the American republic. The historical function of civil society may be described as a non-political area of transactions among citizens, in contradistinction (in the West) to the state (guardian of the common good), and to the church (guide of the soul and morals). Hence civil society was hardly ever institutionalized. Although it functioned with its own intrinsic rules—as in the case of medieval artisan- and trade-corporations (guilds) and throughout history according to the rules and interests of transport, production, distribution, banking, etc.—it was in a sense mistrusted and controlled. The state limited its activities, insofar as in traditional societies its transactions were often entrusted to a certain category of people: *meteikoi* in ancient Greece, which means "outside the household," that is, non-citizens, temporarily admitted foreigners; *vaisyas* in India (tradesmen, artisans, people standing below the priestly and warrior castes); and Syrians and Jews in early medieval Europe. Later the state and the church placed other kinds of controls on economic activity by outlawing high interest rates (usury), limiting market days and places, and advising the higher classes against engaging in commerce and financial speculation.

The Rise of Civil Society

Modern times, in contrast, have been characterized by the rise, expansion, and ideological self-affirmation of civil society.

Economic transactions, immeasurably augmented by industrial productivity (land value fell correspondingly, thus the forms of wealth changed), have profited by an elaborated liberal ideology and by contract theories linking citizens to one another and to the state. The contract (and so civil society) was at the heart of the political philosophy of Hobbes, Grotius, Locke, and Rousseau, while liberalism (see n. 5) became the accepted ideal in its proposal of a new, hardly Catholic definition of morality and the common good. These two were henceforth regarded as the product of the many individual, mostly economic, endeavors which, although the intrinsic orientation of each may be self-seeking, balance out statistically as an adequately (pragmatically) functioning public morality, independent of the teaching of religion. Those who contributed most to the formulation of the liberal pragmatic view were Mandeville, Adam Smith, and John Locke.

The church has always objected to this outlined concept of the common good and public morality. It is thus not surprising that the church is targeted for neutralization, while civil society wants to harness the state to its own interests. We observe the consequence: the state, as an agency of civil society, is tossed back and forth as an overburdened performer of myriad interests. Civil society offers to it, as well as to the church, a *modus vivendi*. The offer to the state, known as the "minimal state," is to be an executant of society's interests through the state's fragmentation into political parties and administrative bureaucracies; the offer to the church is the status of a "service agency," ministering to those who happen to be marginalized by society's dynamic processes: the homeless, the sick (now especially AIDS patients), the minorities, those in need of charity, the orphans, and in general the so-called weak souls wanting a father figure and a reassurance in things not of this world. Looked at dispassionately, triumphant civil society wishes to limit and circumscribe the traditional function of state and church, assigning to them certain areas of activity that in the past formed only a narrow field of their tasks, responsibilities, and mission. In sum, a redistribution has occurred in the triangular relationship of state, civil society, and church. No attention has been paid to these changed roles among political scientists, sociologists, politicians, or churchmen.

Yet the issue is worth considering, since after the separation of church and state we now face the next logical step, the *separation of church and society*, at least in the decision-making sectors of society. It should be clear that we do not describe here a conspiratorial design on the part of civil society. As always in the vast and significant movements of history, we detect multiple causes and perhaps inextricable chains of events in the growth, expansion, and conquests of society. As we have mentioned it, civil society in its elementary forms emerged as a power in the communes of Europe (the city-states of Italy were the first, with their Mediterranean and cross-continental trade), then increased its activity and importance through a power game, with advantages derived from the rivalry of princes, kingdoms, and ecclesiastical authority. The later medieval towns (all over Europe by approximately 1450) began to assert their municipal and financial weight (their city halls and cathedrals are eloquent symbols of this situation), but not before the rise of industry and capitalism did they acquire recognized power status. The thinkers we mentioned—the first being Grotius and Hobbes—gave the first philosophical and legal recognition of the vast transformation that was taking place to the advantage of civil society.

In the second half of the twentieth century the church seems to have finally accepted its reduced influence, although a little over a century ago Pius IX published his *Syllabus of Errors* (1864), anathematizing those who advocated concessions to, and compromises with, liberal ideology. Today it may be said that while doctrinally the church's opposition to liberalism (not to civil society as such) has been maintained, de facto the church has adjusted itself to the social and cultural situation that liberal modernity has created, even though this implies the church's marginalization. The new attitude of the church may be explained by several motives; we shall choose some that seem to have been decisive. The Enlightenment, after weakening considerably the faith of elites, soon combined with the Industrial Revolution which in turn displaced large masses, upsetting their habits of life and belief. This social upheaval led to a situation in which the church had to fear the departure of large categories of people, entire classes who chose a different intellectual, cultural, and material orientation.

The first major loss occurred in the eighteenth century when the widening and increasingly powerful bourgeois class began listening to thinkers and writers like Spinoza, Hobbes, Mandeville, Locke, Voltaire, Diderot, and others. New interests arose: large-scale financial operations about merchandise from the colonies, freemasonry and its penetration of public opinion, clubs and societies where free thinkers and deists congregated to debate philosophical and public issues, with the conclusions of the first applied to the second in the form of political programs. Religious faith and doctrine was less and less able to contain these new aspirations.

The second loss, in the nineteenth century, was the near total desertion from the church of the working class, which associated the church with aggressive and cruel capitalism.[6] The urbanized masses, freshly uprooted from their villages and the influence of the parish priest, now were organized for industrial efficiency and protected by workers' associations. Their moral perception also changed: vice became part of city life, no longer punished by God and community.

Simply put, the church is now determined not to lose out on the spirit of the twentieth century which is largely "classless," amorphous, and much more difficult to describe and locate in its essential concentrations and attitudes than was true in the past. In the eyes of both sociologists and ecclesiastics the problem has become how conceptually to reduce our mobile societies to determinable categories, and then how to evaluate their trends and aspirations.

The Church in Modern Society

The adaptation to modern society underway today in the church—from the Vatican down to parish priests, with bishops and theologians in the lead—is not the result of a haphazard decision. Among the motives we may even find the maturation of an ideal whose roots are found in the writings of St. Augustine. The best minds among those effecting this adaptation to the modern world have hoped indeed to bridge the Augustinian gap between the *civitas Dei* and the *civitas terrena*,

---

6. Such was the case in Europe. In America, economic dynamism raised the question of socialism and atheism only marginally. Besides, masses of immigrants from whom the workers were recruited were sufficiently permeated by religious beliefs to perpetuate the guiding functions of their priests.

a dream as old as Christianity and responsible for many an attempt at utopian solutions, the establishment of the kingdom of God here on earth and within history. The Augustinian hope—not something explicit in the books of the great bishop of Hippo but eagerly seized upon by readers "between the lines"—was that man will cease exploiting his fellows and justice will reign. For this to happen, the spirit of social fraternity will permeate the state itself, which is in Augustine's mind a band of robbers without justice.

The early fathers of the church were certainly not proponents of utopias; they knew that the "kingdom is not of this world," and that no ideal state of affairs is possible this side of the Last Judgment. Their successors—popes, bishops, theologians—remained firmly convinced that not much improvement can be made in human nature and society, and that both must be submitted to the discipline of law, institutions, consecrated tradition, and to the prestige of theologians who accept the church's magisterium in moral matters. The twentieth-century descendants of these men either do not think that way or are persuaded that the contemporary situation is so different from any other situation known in history that an altogether new attitude must be adopted by the church vis-à-vis the world. This much was obvious during visits by John Paul II on American soil when many bishops and laypeople explained to him that the United States and its democratic methods are incompatible with the church's dictation of only one moral truth.

The critique is not new; every century has tried to tell the church how to redefine its doctrine and structure. The spokesmen for such adjustments to the zeitgeist, today called *aggiornamento,* each time believe that the formulas of adaptation they recommend would save the church from public indifference and social marginalization. Some of the outstanding critics in the last 150 years were Lamennais, Loisy, Bultmann, Teilhard de Chardin, Hans Küng, and Schillebeeckx; by offering their own improved and updated version of what Christ taught, and by adapting it to the "demands of the times," they thought that the road they at times vehemently suggested was the way of survival for the church. Pope John's initiative may have been similarly motivated, and after him the ecclesiastical and mundane policies of Paul VI. The thesis today is that in order not to "lose" modern man the way 18th- and 19th-century man was lost, the church needs to adapt to the scientific, technological, democratic, and pluralistic age. The difficulty is, however, that the process of adaptation cannot be stopped at any point; demands follow one another from new sources, encouraged by the eventual success of other demands. Besides, if changes are debated within the existing structures, those outside these structures clamor either for admission or for the demolition of the structures themselves. In other words, once the church is seen as abandoning its firm hold on matters pertaining to doctrine, sacraments, tradition, and magisterium, once it is seen as hesitating, unsure of its conduct, and lax on authority, the direction and rhythm of adaptation are taken out of its hands and passed on to the agencies of civil society. The problem is not so much adaptation, since every living body or institution assimilates parts of its surrounding; the problem is the content and the dimensions of adjustment, the preservation of all the essentials of doctrine and morals and of the traditional guardianship over them.

This is why the previous questions as to whether the post-conciliar upheaval represents adaptation or revolution are legitimate questions. True, "adaptation" is a phenomenon of all times. In the Middle Ages lord bishops had their feudal privileges and opulent lifestyles; abbés in eighteenth-century French salons were not a whit distinguishable from other young bewigged and powdered busybodies; and between the two Renaissance prelates were preoccupied with ancient Hellas, speaking and writing of Venus, Cupid, Apollo, and Jove, swearing by "the Olympian gods" and spending fortunes on ancient statues and vases. What nevertheless preserved the church from secularization[7] was, in addition to a majority of

---

7. The term "secularization" has recently become quite controversial. There are those, including the Islamologist Henry Corbin in France and Peter Berger in this country, who argue that Christianity's predisposition to meddle

upright, often saintly priests and bishops, an unchallenged theological and doctrinal orthodoxy, evident by the exclusion from the ecclesia of such movements and teachings that conflicted with tradition and with the *consensus fidelium* (characterized by St. Vincent of Lerins in the fifth century as "what is believed always, everywhere, and by all"). The doctrinal edifice on which popes and councils were leaning was solid in spite of the sharp debates arbitrated by pontifical authority— *Roma locuta est; causa finita est* (Once Rome speaks, the matter is settled), Augustine had said. Whether it was the philosophy of Aristotle or Averroes (12th and 13th centuries) that had penetrated the theologians' minds, or relatively minor matters threatening the unanimity of faith and its artistic representation,[8] the appropriate authority was ever able to take steps, stem the tide, pronounce a firm *Sic* or a firm *Non*. The road back from error was well lit.

Another factor that has preserved the church from an excessive adjustment to forms of lay society, its fashions, habits, mores, and beliefs, was its sharing of power over society with the state. In this age when power is seen as diffuse and the power elites are camouflaged (as a tribute to democracy), it is hard for us to imagine that state and church were actually dominant factors and that the temporal and spiritual power they held was a meaningful expression of reality. Beyond their numerous conflicts, church and state were in agreement on some essential common interests and endeavors aimed at society's orderliness, at protecting it from internal and external attempts to dissolve it in anarchy. In a famous gospel episode, Jesus recognized the legitimacy of the state (whose history,

---

with secular life (history, society, economy) makes it vulnerable to secular influences. Islam calls this *hudlul,* which means the incarnational aspect of Christianity by which no sacred distance is preserved between God and human preoccupations.

8. See the controversy in the eighteenth century about the legitimacy of representing the Holy Spirit as a seductive young man, instead of the traditional dove. The dove was chosen by Pope Benedict XIV, in 1745. (Francois Boespflug, *Dieu dans l'art: Sollicitudini Nostrae de Benôit XIV (1745) et l'affaire Crescence de Kaufbeuren* [Editions du Cerf, 1984].)

after all, antedated the foundation of the church), and St. Paul underlined this legitimacy when he made use of his Roman citizenship before Governor Felix. The early church gratefully seized the emperor's extended hand, and even before, in the times of persecution, the church fathers and bishops were fully aware of Rome's achievement as a protector and organizer of a civilized commonwealth, and thus of the existence of Christian communities too. Incidentally, while not a few imperial governors and judges showed cruelty to Christians rounded up by police, equally frequent were the cases when officials made attempts at saving the victims' lives by facilitating and simplifying the gesture of compulsory worship before the emperor's effigy.

Later, during the Christian centuries, from the fifth to the seventeenth, innumerable conflicts arose between church and state: popes and emperors fought epic battles for jurisdiction over clergy, for property rights, for primacy in public matters. As a symbolic illustration of this rivalry, one may cite the long habit of papal processions in which the pontiffs wore royal paraphernalia, while on ceremonial occasions kings were bedecked with the insignia of the spiritual power. Still, in matters of preserving the common good and public order the motives of their actions usually coincided. Again, one example: the crusade to wipe out the Albigensian (Catharist) heresy saw the cooperation of the church and the temporal power, since the Cathars, with their Gnostic and Manichaean worldview, rebelled against Rome *and* also against the principles sustaining society: marriage, procreation, institutions, and the orderly functioning of civil existence.[9]

Without doubt the coming of modern society, which with its liberal-democratic spirit and values emphasizes its philosophical opposition to state and church and has effected their

9. The church understood at the same time the need for reaching the marginal members of society. The new reforms, starting with the tenth century (against simony, concubinage, etc.), were followed by a new apostolate aiming at the heretical movements; the Dominican and Franciscan orders came into existence. In a later chapter we shall discuss the contemporary forms of the apostolate among the new marginals.

separation, and in a certain manner their isolation, has placed the church in an altogether novel situation. The liberal program, now nearly universal in the Western world, has an agenda for the church different from its traditional role and mission. The liberal commitment which produced contemporary society has sacralized the secular/industrial democracy and has mobilized powerful counterforces against religion. In the eyes of liberal spokesmen—John Dewey, Margaret Mead, Franz Boas, Bernard Russell—mankind's great hope was that the improved conditions of the masses and the final (after a Marxian phase) emancipation of intellectuals would cause religion to fade away or at least to be absorbed in "normal" social transactions. The belief was that the newly won freedom, prosperity, and commitment to science as a final answer to ultimate questions would demonstrate the uselessness of religion, at least in its institutional form, as well as its inability to cope with the coming world. Only a few years ago Herman Kahn and Alan Wiener predicted the character of the future civilization as "empirical, this-worldly, secular, humanistic, pragmatic, utilitarian, contractual, epicurean or hedonistic."[10] This suggests the belief on the part of an important sector of our intellectuals that the dominant form of our liberal civilization—in reality, a description of America's current convictions and lifestyle—is here to stay. But it also suggests its fragility: would mankind's mastery over its own destiny (the essence of liberal dogma) culminate in mere permissiveness on a gigantic scale? However disappointing a perspective, no doubt many Catholic thinkers also make it their own.[11]

This amounts to an ambiguity vis-à-vis liberalism as the church at least unofficially looks at it. In the last century—the

10. In Peter Berger, *A Rumor of Angels: Modern Society and the Rediscovery of the Supernatural* (Garden City, N.Y.: Doubleday, 1969), p. 1.

11. There are passages in Hans Küng's *On Being a Christian* in which he equates the Christian message with that of the Enlightenment, of the French Revolution, of the scientific worldview. Other Catholic opinion leaders argue for sexual permissiveness. There is in fact hardly a contemporary proposition formulated by sectors or spokesmen of civil society that is not at once taken up by a theologian, professor, or bishop and packaged in some Christian terminology.

time when the *Syllabus* indirectly countered Darwin's and
Spencer's influence[12]—the church reacted strongly against
liberalism because only one class, the bourgeoisie, advocated
it. To the extent that liberal *society* prevailed over the traditional *state* (also through the extension of the bourgeoisie as a
universal class), important Catholic thinkers began dismissing
the *Syllabus* as an obscurantist document transcended by
evolving Catholic thought. What happened between the
middle of the last century and the middle of this one is that
liberalism has become a social orthodoxy and the entire apparatus of modern society has come to be considered the
embodiment of an unquestioned truth, a cultural final word
concerning the individual and the public weal. Just as the
church adjusted in many respects to the feudal, then to the
absolute-monarchist, order and civilization, it adapts itself in
our century to the liberal-democratic system and its cultural
style. Peter Berger points out in *The Sacred Canopy* that for
moderns the facts of the social milieu acquire the unquestion-
able reality of the facts of nature; men and women are surrounded by society the way they are by the physical universe.
For us in this century, liberal democracy, science and industry,
consumerism and advertisement—the combined cultural impact of all of these—are as much a part of the environment as
were, in centuries past, the givens of land cultivation, the
feudal order, or society's hierarchical structure.

It appears that in the eyes of many churchmen and
Catholic intellectuals the church has been tied to the old order
of things and not truly updated, in spite of the efforts of the
Second Vatican Council. What do these charges mean to these
Catholic opinion-leaders? They mean that liberal society is not
merely one passing phase in the constantly changing course of
civilizations, but is a kind of terminal for the locomotive of
history—the point of arrival, an absolute, beyond which there
is no further and incalculable vista, or, if you wish, only further

---

12. Darwin's and Spencer's age was, however, also that of Donoso
Cortés, Cardinal Newman, Lord Acton, and Montalembert. These Catholic
thinkers were and are much less known than the first mentioned.

versions of the same "today."[13] We find this conviction about the permanence of the present social forms in Kahn's and Wiener's "scientific" prediction, and in the new researches and conclusions of futurology and prospectivism. They are understandable attempts to arrest time, similar in motivation and scope to the ceremonies of archaic tribes which aim at the recapture of ancient moments of collective memory. It seems that modern society with its immensely powerful publicity apparatus has succeeded in persuading itself that the general conditions of existence have become so perfected that the human condition is now nearing its abolition and that openness ("transparence"), contentment, and perpetual prosperity may become a scientifically guaranteed state of affairs. Why not then urge the church to adjust to society and its dominant norms, judged superior to the so far accepted norms of the church?

Many suggestions arise out of the contemporary milieu as to how the church may start on the road of adaptation, but all of them take for granted that the adaptation should be unilateral. As Fr. Louis Bouyer wrote, "The idea has surfaced that the church has no business converting the world but must itself convert to it; it has nothing to teach the world, only obediently listen to its message."[14] Society is not summoned to observe Christian values; it is the church which is supposed to transform itself on the secular model. The reason for this lopsided program is that the modern world sees itself as a counter-church, superior to the other, and thus an object worthy of imitation. Several powerful ideologies responsible for our contemporary situation were considered exclusive models, potentially new churches. Hegel's philosophy was one, Auguste Comte's positivist system another. Huxleyan evolutionism, Nietzsche's cult of the superman, Marx's classless

13. This is what philosopher Eric Voegelin called the "immanentization of the eschaton," the belief that what Christianity regards as the ultimate manifestation of Christ is taking place now, or soon, in history, as a consequence of a secular system of salvation.

14. Louis Bouyer, *La décomposition du catholicisme* (Aubier-Montaigne, 1968).

society—all preached to the church a conversion to their own worldviews and agendas. The upshot of these efforts and ideologies is that the church and the faith it has taught and represented, and on which it has staked its existence since St. Paul, have gradually lost plausibility.

Disaffection in High Places

What accounts for this lack of credibility that affects not only the church but also the entire institutional and value framework with which the church is associated in the minds of opinion-leaders, whether politicians, media men, university professors, or spokesmen for vast bureaucracies? On the level of ordinary people, cracks in the old system appear when it no longer offers them shelter—that is, a collection of explanations and intellectual and emotional certitudes. Religion, always the highest and most general system of certitudes, is also the last to suffer from the blows of rival systems, since it is not within everyone's speculative ability to connect the religious truth in which they believe with the new propositions challenging this truth. But under the impact of competing systems the traditional answers are gradually eroded and replaced by other answers, perceived as more plausible, better responses to questions people implicitly ask in their daily existence. The "real" that the old system satisfactorily defined suddenly appears as a vacillating illusion, an error, an unexamined notion. A new "real" takes its place, perhaps subsuming the old one as a subclass.

Now something of this sort may have happened to the church when it was challenged by modern worldviews and sensitivities. The process of the "collision" will not be detailed here further. It is important to keep in mind, however, that the essential condition of survival for a belief system or idea complex is that its chief representatives unconditionally believe in its truth and possess the qualities of keeping the system together and viable. The early church possessed such individuals, and even though we call many of them *saints* they were also *statesmen* with a strong vision and faith-inspired strength of action as thinkers, organizers, builders, gatherers, and leaders of men. Truth as such does not move masses and centuries. Transcending both, the representatives of truth must be exceptionally forceful individuals, not afraid of authority when it is exercised for the safeguarding of truth as they see and live it. St. Bernard and St. Catherine of Siena did not hesitate to upbraid popes, sternly reminding them that by not using the authority bestowed on them by Christ they are more than derelict—they are sinners. Again, a statement by Fr. Bouyer will help us to discern the crucial issue: the individual, he writes, is provided by society with various methods to stave off the nightmare world of anomy (lawlessness in moral matters, lack of rules and guideposts) and to stay within the safe boundaries of the established law.[15] Let us put "church" in the place of "society": the believer is equipped by his church with points of doctrine, articles of faith, sacred texts for prayer, sacraments, a language rendered sacred by long use and unchanged meanings, rituals at every station of life—all of these culminating in the encounter with God at the altar. Everything contrary to this belief system signifies non-faith, assault on morality, the symbols of a godless abyss. The believer is so safe in the universe of faith guaranteed to him by God's presence and his commandments that outside challenge cannot move him. But when his own leaders—persons touched directly by the sacred—begin to vacillate and slip away from the central truth, individual faith will have difficulty standing up to the winds of anomy; if it does, its own relative fragility becomes obvious: the Catholic church is a corporation hierarchically structured: flaws and fissures in the edifice affect the whole construction.

Thus the modern onslaught against the church culminates in disaffection in high places. The visible and striking thing in the eyes of Catholics and non-Catholics alike is the rapidity and eagerness with which changes are carried out. These changes are eagerly justified, with something like the

15. Bouyer, p. 24.

following arguments: This is not apostasy but an updating, a deeper grasp of the faith with its implications, a generous communion with other people and religions; such an adjustment, the argument continues, must be couched in a new terminology—that of science, of the jargon of youth, of so far voiceless minorities, of irresistible movements like feminism, and so on. However, this new kind of *apologia* becomes less convincing when intimidated American bishops plead for altar girls, when pressure groups clamor for women priests and a married clergy, and when a theologian announces that "the very notion of salvation coming from God is an insult to the world that modern man cannot accept."[16]

Incentives to adjust have been furnished by a long line of Catholic thinkers whose main concern was to have the church accepted by the modern world. The "modern world" did not, however, have the same regard for these critics. Some—the *Esprit* group in France, Emmanuel Mounier's personalism, the worker-priest movement, Dorothy Day's followers in America—saw the church's future as necessarily harmonious with socialism, even the Marxian kind. Others, Jacques Maritain, for example, found in American society the ideal place for the practice of evangelical virtues because he thought that in this democracy there would be no interference with forms of worship by state or society. Maritain and Fr. John Courtney Murray thus argued that liberal democracy is the regime closest to what a Christian civilization may produce in the temporal order of things. In the post-1945 collective exuberance, liberal democratic society could indeed appear, in opposition to totalitarianism, as an ideal form of society where all legitimate aspirations may be satisfied. Even in the sixties, as many testify, the postwar enthusiasm continued unabated, with new expectations—hoped-for changes in post-Stalinist Russia; decolonization; the presidency of a Catholic in the United States; soaring technology and space travel; the hopes attached to the United Nations, now enlarged with dozens of new members; the convocation of the Vatican Council—all of which could be

16. Bouyer.

interpreted as signposts of a triumphant worldwide liberal program. The German Reformed theologian Jürgen Moltmann shared and described this climate of exhilaration.

The question arises in our day, however, whether the church may really be reconciled with liberal-secular values, a point that Fr. Murray was compelled to ask in the face of disquieting changes in the basic assumptions of American society, which until the sixties were held to be self-evidently true. In other words, was the hypothesis formulated by liberals from Tocqueville to Maritain verifiable when it insisted that the church, separated from the state, would automatically find a shelter under the vast dome of civil society, and that, in turn, it would stand by as society's guardian in moral matters and as a decent public philosophy? What if liberalism, and modernity in general, remained hostile to the church even after church and state separated? In that case, the church, no matter how thoroughly it pursues its "adaptation," would not find tranquility within civil society and through integration with its groups, but would continue to be regarded as both an anachronism and an irritant. It would even be the target of renewed attacks.

Attacks do not mean persecution (although the separating line is often very thin), but rather a policy of marginalization, diminution of influence, and moral limitation contrary to the mission of the church. Concretely, how should the church respond when, under pressure from interest groups protected by liberal-pluralist policy, legislators pass laws opposed to church teaching (on such issues as divorce, abortion, parental approval of teenage abortion, surrogate motherhood, artificial insemination, homosexuality, pornography, etc.)?[17] To be sure, it may oppose such laws (the characteristic term is *lobbying*), but when they are passed by a majority, ought the church to behave like any other group in a pluralistic society, and submit; or ought it to reject the law, referring to a higher one, that of its Founder?[18] All in all, the question is whether the church has

17. The recent (1987) Vatican *Instructions* on these issues point out their incompatibility with church teaching.

18. In the United States natural law is not taught in most law schools, only positive law in the spirit of Justice Oliver Wendell Holmes and Prof. Hans

gained anything in accepting the demotion from partnership with the state to partnership with (liberal) society? Naturally the church did not choose but inherited the condition common to all citizens. The American church does not fall in line only with the other groups, but also with the country's new Catholic bourgeoisie which is sorely tempted, indeed increasingly permeated, by the ruling secular humanism and its values.[19] Yet the question concerning benefits or drawbacks for the church, derived from adaptation to civil society, must be raised; it is crucial for the future.

Kelsen. It is doubtful whether law students trained to regard only positive law as valid are endowed with insight into the notion of divine law.

19. See for example the recent Buffalo opinion poll among Catholics. On questions about women priests, married clergy, sexual ethics, etc., those who approve the "liberal" agenda represent about 40 percent, those who disapprove about 20 percent. Those with no opinion amount to 40 percent. This means that there is as of now a potential majority of Catholics strongly influenced by liberal Protestantism and secular humanism.

CHAPTER TWO

Deconstruction

From the beginning of Western Christian history there have been three major players in the political arena. In the temporal order of things power is sought by all organized political participants; the Western method of achieving and distributing power is distinguished from power seeking in other societies and civilizations by the fact that competitors are not eliminated; their rights and chances are recognized. When Jesus, confronted with a Roman coin, commanded that power be shared between the spiritual and the temporal he laid down a new law and formulated a new mentality that was to stamp all future Christian commonwealths. This did not by any means exclude conflict between church and state, a conflict that fluctuated throughout subsequent centuries. Yet the principle of duality was taken for granted, and neither state nor church sought to eliminate the other. It remains only a question of how much power? Over what part of society should it be exercised? And by what methods?

To simplify a complex story, between the two conflicting and cooperating institutions a third one, civil society, emerged, often profiting by the weakness of one protagonist, and just as often making demands that neither could deny.[1] Civil society

---

1. In the summary of sociologist Jean Duvignaud, for several centuries the medieval towns, made up of burghers, artisans, fugitives from estates, and settled tradesmen, gathered in communes (originally meaning "oaths") and played a kind of twofold role between the existing powers and institutions.

sought a place under the sun through such means as economic power and wealth, the binding nature of contracts, the territorial rights of burghers, and laws formulated so as to favor municipal expansion. If we are to characterize the Renaissance, we might suggest that it was the crucial time when state, church, and society achieved (through a series of conflicts and compromises) an equilibrium: all three attained roughly equal power, though each tried to accumulate more power than the others, attempts that took the forms of (*a*) royal absolutism, (*b*) Counter Reformation, and (*c*) capitalism.

There was nothing unusual in this, and for a long time the "arrangement" did not mean the breakup of the *christiana respublica*. After all, the Roman empire had not broken up either; on the contrary, it had gained two more centuries of life when in A.D. 313 Constantine associated the church to his imperial power. It is part of human affairs that power is respected and its contribution solicited. In 313, the empire was relatively weak, and the church strong, having weathered the persecutions. At the Renaissance, then increasingly afterwards, civil society was perceived by contemporaries as the growing power, notwithstanding the appearances which favored the prestige of the absolute monarchy and of the post–Counter Reformation church. Another two centuries passed, and at the threshold of the French Revolution the abbé Sieyès asked and answered the question: "What is the Third Order (the bourgeoisie)?" The answer: "Everything!" The church had asked for less in 313, but, like the bourgeoisie in 1789, it had received much.

Civil society gradually acquired political power through the insight in the seventeenth century that wars and passions can only be curbed with the help of the equally strong impulse of economic interests. Passions and interests (the title of sociologist Albert O. Hirschman's illuminating work), like wars and conquests, wear each other out, and at the end the peaceful ambitions of getting rich by industry and commerce will elim-

---

These towns were strongholds of solidarity, although they soon had to face division, between property owners and the developing urban proletariat.

inate aggression, both domestically (the social contract) and among nations (permanent peace). The place of the military hero was gradually taken by the trader, and a stable society was sought (Mandeville, Montesquieu, Adam Smith) through a state so dependent on commerce and economic endeavors that it could not risk the citizens' prosperity by launching wars. Montesquieu himself wrote: "The spirit of commerce brings with it the spirit of frugality, economy, moderation, work, wisdom, tranquility, order, regularity. As long as this spirit prevails, the riches it creates do not have any bad effect."[2] The transformation from one social value system to the other brought forth and formulated the liberal civil society whose predominance was assured over the state, which was seen as abusive and aggressive, and over the church, which was seen as a shelter of old, antisocial values.

We established in chapter 1 that civil society and liberal ideology have become linked, generating and strengthening each other. Facing hierarchical orders like state and church, the agenda of civil society was to weaken (for radicals, to abolish) the Throne and the Altar. This was indeed the program of the Enlightenment *philosophes*—level the ranks of spiritual and temporal authority, distribute power among newly created institutions, and elevate the economic principle ("political economy" was its first label) to a position of social and cultural arbitration. Insofar as this program was implemented, civil society in the last two centuries has gradually overshadowed the two other powers and assigned to them new roles within national communities. Nobody can tell at this apogee of civil society's power how state and church, the other components of the historical "triangle," will evolve in the future. But since Western mobility is not only social and economic but also political and cultural, new configurations should not be considered impossible, although it is within human nature to assume that the momentary power holder believes that his place at the summit is forever assured. Power and its concentration and influence are anchored in the nature of things, although our age

2. Montesquieu, *The Spirit of the Laws*, V, 7.

is particularly sanguine about the denial of this truth. As Louis Dumont writes in *Homo hierarchicus*, "hierarchy is at the heart of the things that are hidden from modern ideology, although it is so universal that it is ready to manifest itself in masked, self-effacing, and pathological forms, as if it were in hiding from popular notions."[3] Yet, simple observation confirms that power in the last 150 years has only shifted from one group to another, where it wears a new mask, uses a new rhetoric, and paints new images on the horizon of society. Under the canopy of liberalism, such concentrations as pressure groups possess substantial power: media, universities, minorities of all kinds, culture figures, and a variety of ideological networks. They possess a quasi-monopoly on interpreting events and movements of ideas, in the manner of dominant classes of all times. Power, after all, is not always military hardware, a given hierarchy, or riches; it is, especially in leveled, democratic societies, the ownership of words and meanings.

Image over Substance

Our discussion now concerns the church's mechanics of adaptation to modern liberal society, a form of "modern apostolate" that involves the church's grasp of the fact that the liberal world requires of it too, as a means of effectiveness, the direct approach, informality, and democratic participation. The "traveling pope," John Paul II, seems to have understood this demand of the age as he meets enormous crowds, kisses babies, converses with folk singers, and lets himself be photographed with a wide grin on his face. The approach is clearly adopted from methods of publicity and from the style of advertising posters, and its ecclesiastical practitioners also submit to the demand for image and the commercial technique. Although the church is not a democratic structure, popes and bishops behave like the spokesmen of democracy who go through the same motions of smiling, kissing, and shaking hands.

3. Louis Dumont, *Homo hierarchicus* (Paris: Gallimard, 1966), pp. 300-301.

The contradiction between the traditionally sacred character of the church and the current behavior of its representatives creates a malaise, a conflict in the minds of believers—not only believers of higher classes and with historical memories, but also simple people who seem to need the contrast between the routine of the workday world and the solemn ceremonies representing the exceptional, the unique, beauty, and mystery. In general, all people associate the manifestations of the sacred—whether person, object, or event—with distance, infrequency, veneration, quiet, and awe. Thus what believers witness now seems to be the banalization of the sacred, the projection of a thousand images, the abolition of distance. As long as this is a novelty popular fervor may double, because now the secrecy of the old sacred combines with the quasi-profane conduct of its habitual guardians. The so far "hidden" sanctuary is suddenly displayed. The combination of previously unlinked elements adds piquancy to ecclesiastical manifestations, just as the addition of rare condiments to accustomed dishes excites the tired palate. Fairly soon, however, this air of ambiguity about the sacred diminishes its credibility, and people turn away from what seem to them un-genuine combinations and, above all, concessions to the zeitgeist.

The ambiguity goes further than the reduction of the sacred to commercial image-making. If images were limited to externalia alone, the believer might reason that these are superficial gestures of adjustment to the habits of industrial civilization, which feeds on images, slogans, and artificial attitudes. Images and slogans are essential parts of a continuing campaign of reassurance for the populace that it is "king" in all matters: consumership, politics, mass culture. The entire modern advertisement industry can be understood as a campaign of flattery directed at the "sovereign people," the pinnacle of democracies. Kings and emperors used to be flattered by depictions of their conquest, praise offered their monuments, assuring signs of their subjects' loyalty. The modern sovereign of liberal-democratic society needs another kind of flattery: all its members, the multitude, the "sovereign," must be told day and night (this is why the role of television is enormous) that everybody is permanently at its beck and call, offering it goods, services, images, sounds, and spectacles.[4]

The flattery addressed to the sovereign people stops here. Beyond the ritual of the productivist-consumerist dance the sovereign people is subjected to a harsh treatment by its managers and manipulators; it is often pressed into service and taken advantage of like a blind king. Yet this does not mean that people are fooled: they play the game as dictated by the myth that sustains society. In the church, however, no myth is needed; there the supernatural is the rock-bottom reality, and the believer needs no flattery. He knows that it is more important that the bishop should wash his feet at Easter than that the pope should shake his hand at an airport. The first gesture is sacred—the believer participates in Christ's original gesture and intent; the second is a concession to the showiness of the mass age. Washing of feet is surrounded by sacred symbols; the handshake at a mass rally is a morsel to the poor from the table of the rich.

Those then to whom the new, democratic ecclesiastical behavior is addressed are plunged into a lukewarm pool of equivocation. Does this behavior at least bring benefits to the church and strength to the faith? It is not necessary to compare the pope's position and attitude today to those of his predecessors in the so-called "ages of faith," the Gregory VIIs, the Innocent IIIs, the Boniface VIIIs.[5] Power relations were very different then; the church is now in the position of a petitioner applying for full membership in civil society, bringing pledges

4. According to Pascal in his *Pensées,* the exceptional status of a king is manifested in the permanent effort of his entourage to provide for his entertainment (distraction). Hardly any better description exists for the "sovereign people" of today, entertained (distracted) day and night by publicity, current events, and television programs.

5. Some passages from the *Determinatio compendiosa* (1342) concerning papal prerogatives: "He is above every council and statute. . . . He has no superior on earth . . . gives dispensation from every law. . . . It is he who alters the substance of a thing. . . . The pope is living law . . . to whom nobody may say 'Why do you do that?'" Quoted in Francis Oakley, *The Western Church in the Later Middle Ages* (Ithaca, N.Y.: Cornell U. Press, 1979), p. 165.

of loyalty[6]—not in the form of tangible tribute, but in the form of words, gestures, and behavior which convey to the power holders of civil society the message that the church accepts the liberal presuppositions and the rules of the game. In fact, the pope's solemn words to the faithful indicate his ambiguous position. He must both criticize liberal society for its hedonism and other sins *and* defend it as a kind of ultimate achievement, a glory of evolution. On the one side is his alarm over the de-Christianization of civil and social life, the legalized sins, the desertion from the Mass and from priesthood and seminaries, the mechanization of birth and death. On such occasions the pope speaks as a pastor, a delegate of Jesus Christ, a prophet denouncing society. On the other side is the tacit acceptance of all these phenomena through the adjustment of the ecclesiastical machinery to contemporary forms of societal existence and to the ideological assumptions behind them. There was the crisis of catechism in France, so grave that Cardinal Ratzinger had to intervene; there is the closing of seminaries for lack of parish placements for priests;[7] the numerical and qualitative depletion of the clergy; theologians rebelling against the whole gamut of Catholic doctrine, their ideas being shaped by fashionable philosophies, temporary hypotheses of science, or the articles of Reformed creed; the centrifugal movements and blatant disobedience of religious orders; the dispute, degenerating to exchange of information about sexual life, over the church's right to prescribe moral duties. In brief, what the pope and an occasional bishop lament is indirectly accepted by the church's tolerant policy and refusal to use authority.

Note that this policy is exactly what liberal ideology prescribes for its own participating interest groups. Let us be

6. In his post-conciliar address to the diplomats accredited to the Vatican, Paul VI said that the church's only desire is to be "a free institution within a free society." This request conforms to the liberal program.

7. There are several reasons that explain this. One is the notion of excessive egalitarianism which tolerates no distinction between functions. The priest's mediating role is thereby excluded, and his special grace is not recognized. Under pressure of democratization priests feel uneasy about their uniqueness. As priests become rare, the "priesthood of the laity" asserts itself, and distinctions are erased.

fair: the church knew many periods in its history when grave ills troubled it. Simony and the concubinage of priests were the internal issues attacked by Gregory VII; heresy in all its forms burdened popes in the 12th and 13th centuries; conciliar defiance of pontifical magisterium was at issue in the 14th; and so on. But in all these cases Rome strongly resisted, and its case finally triumphed. Today, the church shies away from pointing at its adversaries; it is on the defensive.[8] Is this a change of style? Such changes usually go deeper than the surface. The style now is "liberal" (as it once was "feudal" or "monarchic"), that of the "open society." In what areas of public life do we find outstanding modifications?

We find them as sutures along lines where the Catholic concept and liberal society meet, fostering a fusion of two worldviews. The penetration is preponderantly, not to say exclusively, that of liberal ideology, which acts as a dissolver of the religious worldview and practice. Let us take our illustrations from the process as it is evolving. It should be noted that in past interactions between church and society the church had the active, impactive role, as it always did in mankind's institutional past; society transformed itself along the guidelines of the church. It is evident, of course, that many other factors contributed to such transformations; yet the leading part fell to the church through its moral discourse.[9] In our time, however, we can no longer speak of even a mutual penetration, but only of a one-sided impact: liberal civil society is today the dominant entity. According to one's point of view, it is either deplorable or fascinating to watch the church's effort at

8. Compare the present sweet words addressed to civil society, but also to dissidents within the church, with the harsh warnings that used to be addressed to the state, the excommunication of rulers, the interdicts on masses of believers for their sins. The point is not whether one or the other is the more reasonable and charitable attitude, but the church's softened attitude vis-à-vis civil society.

9. Moral discourse and a degree of legislative coercion in the name of the common good. A good illustration is provided in the effort of the church for more than a century in feudal society to reject concubinage and recognize children born in wedlock. The moral aspect was joined to order in family and property relations.

mimicry as it adjusts to liberal society: its mentality, discourse, and self-structuring.

What Has Happened to the Priest?

The phenomenon of adjustment takes place on several levels and, quite understandably, what these levels shall be is determined by civil society. In other words, it is not a process of mutual accommodation, but of imitation and adaptation to a dominant model. According to the ideology of civil society in our time the adjusting institution is expected to become *democratic* in mentality and structure; *pluralist* in its acceptance of other institutions, groups, and movements as equals; and *ecumenical* in its reformulation of its vocation, reserving an important place for other creeds that share, outwardly at least, its own preoccupations.

What about the church's recently inaugurated *democratization?* Corresponding to the secular concept of the "sovereign people," Vatican II brought forth from its debates the notion of the "people of God" as a collective name for all believers, potentially extensible also to non-Catholics, as theologian Karl Rahner's category of "anonymous Christians" (which includes atheists) suggests. It is not merely renewed terminology; it is the basis for a restructuring of the *ecclesia*. The sociological justification is at hand: the transformation of cities into centers of industrial and endlessly expanding urban development has made the traditional parish structure obsolete. In the modern industrial milieu members of a neighborhood no longer know each other. The social-industrial mobility displaces them frequently, bringing new residents as old ones move away to similarly mobile and ephemeral places like the modern suburb. The parish as a unit is declared to be a thing of the past, and the dynamic elements among new residents are supposed to cohere in other types of organizations.

But the real issue is elsewhere. Do the new "base communities," as new associations are now increasingly called, need a priest? Insofar as the new communities consist of modern, mobile, up-to-date professionals they are regarded as re-

ligiously self-sufficient (the term used is "mature"), sociologically advanced over old parishes whose members were used to
the traditional ways. Karl Rahner, at the forefront of the updating of the church, has written that the new objective ought to
be the conversion of urban intellectuals; "old women lighting
candles in village churches" may be considered remnants.
Behind Rahner's judgment is the view that there are, as it were,
two religions: the old meaning of the faith was passive acceptance, subordination to a hierarchy whose immediately available lowest echelon is the parish priest; and the updated
meaning, the democratically organized "people of God," where
equality diminishes the importance of the hierarchy and thus
the function of the priest as mediator: between God and man,
between bishop and community (ex-parish), and eventually
between the people of God and Rome. According to this logic,
which today increasingly is accredited as the shape of things
for tomorrow, any layman (thus why not laywoman?) may
fulfill the sacerdotal function, sharing its various aspects with
other members of the community, including non-Catholics.
The priest himself is scheduled to turn into a bureaucrat, an
auxiliary person with unspecified contributions to the life of
the base community.

Many call this process "protestantization." In places
where this process has been implemented—in France, for
example—it involves the socialization and consequent religious neutralization of the priest, and eliminates him as a
mediator. It once was assumed that through ordination the
priest became a sacred person, touched by Christ through the
instrumentality of the ordaining bishop. As the story of Moses
on Mount Sinai showed, the awe before the face of God was
not to be sustained by the believers—it had to be mediated to
them by an intercessor who served as a channel for the sacred
and for the validation of sacraments. Moses represented the
people on Sinai, where he obtained the Decalogue. The Levites
and Cohanites formed a priestly class in the Israelite community, similar to the priestly caste among Indo-European tribes
and societies. The priest thus always stood out and apart,
marked by his sacred function and the mystery of mediation.

But a society in which the sacred and the awe surrounding it have been eroded needs no mediators. This erosion was preprogrammed by liberal ideology, and its exclusive reliance on the individual and his rational faculty makes the sacred component of religion appear not only a gratuitous fantasy of our emotional side, but also a humiliation. After all, as a denial of equality among the people of God, it challenges the freedom American citizens enjoy in picking and choosing convenient doctrinal and moral truths. The vanishing practice of confession before communion suggests, to be sure, the confusion introduced in sacramental life, but it also points to the phasing out of priestly functions. Sacraments, interpreted as acts of friendship among men rather than a communion with God, become a horizontal link in an increasingly secular network; thus they can be administered outside the consecrating forms, inspired by the emotions of the moment and the style of circumstances.[10]

The lack of parishes and the emptying of seminaries are therefore largely a pseudo-problem. There are fewer priests not because other professions and occupations tempt young men away from the priesthood but because candidates are made to feel they are superfluous in a "mature" society. The so-called experts, lay and ecclesiastic, then use the paucity of priests as a pretext for occupying influential positions inside and vis-à-vis the church and redirecting its mission. This is how Cardinal Ratzinger diagnosed the situation, extending his analysis beyond the case discussed here: "On the one hand, active orders and congregations are in a grave crisis: the discovery of professionalism, the concept of social welfare which has replaced that of 'love of neighbor', the often uncritical and yet enthusiastic adaptation to the new and hitherto unknown values of modern secular society . . . of psychologies and psychoanal-

10. The increasing association of laymen to the sacramental function is bound to alter the nature of the sacraments. There are countries where the scarcity of priests prompts the setting up of "Assemblies in the Absence of Priests." For weeks there are no priests to visit parishes and celebrate Mass; thus inevitably modified forms of worship, stamped by individual subjective inspiration will become the rule, varying from one community to another.

yses of different tendencies: all of this had led to burning problems with identity and, with many women, to the collapse of motivations sufficient to justify religious life."[11]

The adjustment of sacred practices and ecclesiastical personnel to liberal society is a sociologically plausible process, and it is indicative of new power relationships. The nineteenth-century French Catholic publicist, Louis Veuillot, whose career coincided in time with the papacy of Pius IX and the publication of the *Syllabus*, described the break between liberal society and the church as one long prepared by liberal ideologues and destined to be definitive. But, Veuillot added, some liberals who are stamped by their Catholic background believe that the break would benefit society at large as well as the church, thereby giving it peaceful relationships with other groups and a great deal of freedom among them, due to a new respect for a church freed from association with power. This expectation is an illusion.

Speaking without Power: The Church in a Pluralistic World

The case that we can label as the church's adaptation to *pluralism* is not so simple as Catholic liberals in Veuillot's time—among them Alexis de Tocqueville—believed it would be. Institutions, even those "not of this world," must either possess a power of their own or be protected by some other power, a principle clearly understood by the fourteenth-century thinker Marsilius of Padua, whose thesis could have enfeebled the church at the time had the papacy not been at the peak of its power and prestige. Marsilius was a "liberal democrat" before that term had been coined, and American scholar Alan Gewirtz actually describes him as one of the ancestors of modern democratic thinking. The church, Marsilius wrote in *Defensor Pacis*, does not constitute a distinct society; it is a part of civil society, but since society had not yet

11. Joseph Ratzinger and Vittorio Messori, *The Ratzinger Report* (San Francisco: Ignatius, 1985), p. 56.

acquired a status of its own in the fourteenth century (though it was on the point of doing so), the church was nothing but an organ of the state, at that time the empire. The state therefore has the right, the Paduan scholar wrote, to fix the number of priests needed, the way it also determines the number of soldiers needed for its defense. Priests obtain their authority from the lay legislators, the limits of which are set by the emperor's jurists. And so on.

This seems to us an extreme case, but let us bear in mind that it is reality under today's Marxist regimes. Liberal societies are more lenient, according to their pluralist credo, but it is pluralism with its indirect and multiple pressures that instills religious indifference in the population. Liberal society offers myriad inducements not only in the form of professional outlets and interesting careers; it also offers and popularizes a style of life which appears irresistible. The magnetism of mundane activities and attitudes and the temptation of choices prompt many ecclesiastics to at least underemphasize their own status and resort to various stratagems in the demonstration of their adherence to the liberal-pluralist spirit. It is impossible, of course, to estimate the number of ecclesiastics who behave ambiguously—just as it would have been impossible to do so in the era of Constantine, when priests and monks were offered exemption from taxes and military service. The issue, however, is that those who today behave in this way present a *type*, the indifferent, cooled-off, even cynical and non-believing ecclesiastic who injects into the area of faith a debilitating element. Many of them would not be caught wearing a cassock; others mention "superstition" when discussing sacraments, or protest when belief in Christ and salvation is attributed to sacraments. The episodes relating to such matters multiply quickly, and indifference among Catholics grows proportionally.

We have pointed out repeatedly that similar phenomena were known in earlier eras too, but that society then offered no shelters to disbelief, at least not in the public square. In the same century when Marsilius launched his attack on the church, the poet-humanist Petrarch wrote in one of his letters that he had just showed the door to a "follower of Averroes" (this meant then an atheist) who was visiting him and conversing with him about the soul's mortality and other such topics. Contrast Petrarch's indignation with the leaning-over-backward attitude of many churchmen today in discussing religious issues at television panels, teaching courses at Catholic universities, publishing books, or commenting on papal encyclicals. Since pluralism implies an "open mind," many are influenced by a wide gamut of sects and movements they join, although such a half-hidden membership may be incompatible with their oath of ordination or simply with their loyalty to the church: Marxism, freemasonry, oriental cults, or secular humanism. The number of scandalous cases is growing where priests refuse to perform baptisms for the newborn, weddings, burials, or last unctions, where they distort the Mass or show contempt for the worshipers' orthodoxy. Your gestures are based on a myth, they say, or suggest a sociological retardation.

From these numerous cases one gathers that the bishops of the Vatican Synod in 1985 were well advised to describe pluralism as "a juxtaposition of systems of belief that are fundamentally opposed to each other"—thus implicitly condemning it—not mentioning, however, that if these systems oppose each other, then for the sake of social peace one or a few will prevail at the expense of the others. One is thus entitled to remain skeptical about the bishops' ability to counter the trend that follows the logic of civil society as it is constituted today.

This logic is manifest in all transactions of society, and has penetrated, ironically, the sessions of the annual Synods themselves. During the Synod that had its sessions in October 1987, American women observers noted the use by participants of terms borrowed not from Catholic documents discussing the place of women in the church, but from radical feminist vocabulary. The meaning given to "sexism," "equality of men and women," "women's liberation," and so on was the same one that ideological parlance has consecrated over the last decade. Church representatives are obviously overwhelmed by these pressures, which show their impact in legislative bodies and the courts. A striking instance occurred when a district

judge struck down the Family Life Act of 1981 that allowed
religious groups (mostly Roman Catholic) the use of federal
money to teach adolescents self-discipline as a form of birth
control. Advising chastity, said the judge in 1987, is a religious
message; thus the use of public funds for it contradicts the
separation of church and state. The case confirms what we
have said about the indirect way in which imposed secular
humanism enjoys a nonreligious status. While Planned Parenthood encourages sex, contraception, and abortion, chastity—
which has been regarded as the highest virtue of all by religions
and civilizations—has its moral worth officially degraded.
Pluralism, therefore, is not even a scrupulously observed technique for equal rights; it may function in favor of an anti-Chris-
tian ideology.

As an official body with a religious mission, the church
does not publicly signify its submission to the tenets of civil
society. Yet we witness a double phenomenon: (1) civil society,
with sectorial demands multiplying daily, overwhelms the
public square and enforces its choices to the detriment of other
choices that by definition are not contained in the secular
framework; and (2), under pressure to conform to civil society's
standards, representatives of the church gradually and willy-
nilly adopt the attitudes of adjustment. Liberal society claims,
of course, that it merely enforces pluralism, and that, as the
essence of freedom, it is not an imposition on any individual
or group. The counter argument, however, is that a purely
formal definition of freedom means the freedom of all points
of view and messages. In the case of such an absolute freedom
the strong repress the weak—in the name of freedom. Thus, in
the "free marketplace of ideas" those ideas which camouflage
themselves as "pluralistic" possess a built-in advantage, really
a privilege. It is evident why the church cannot thus camouflage itself, that is, claim that it is internally pluralistic—but
also why many of its representatives are desperately trying to
blend in, while others have persuaded themselves that pluralism would indeed be a good thing for the church's structural
and (why not?) credal reorganization. This point, the latest
temptation of the kingdom of this world, is at the heart of the

church's present crisis: How to turn the church into a copy of pluralist civil society?

Pluralist civil society has its built-in logic which it follows in its own downward spiral. The Jesuit Francis Canavan calls the logic "an endless but fruitless search for the lowest common denominator that can serve as society's moral bond." Canavan's illustration is taken from the history of America: "We did away with state churches in this country so that all Protestants could feel at home in it. We de-Protestantized the country so that Catholics too, could feel at home in it. We have dechristianized the country to make Jews feel welcome, then de-religionized it so that atheists and agnostics may feel equally welcome. Now we are de-moralizing the country so that deviants from accepted moral norms will not feel excluded. The lowest common denominator is like the horizon, always approached but never reached."[12]

Many privatized groups contend for power on the plain of the common denominator, but the strength of any one is curbed by the presence of the others. This plurality of privatized groups is ideally suited for business enterprises which easily and comfortably submit to the rules of the marketplace: competition, publicity, the presentation of new products, and sales campaigns. Privatization affects the church's function very differently. The church's "dynamic" was formulated and given meaning by its founder. It consists of baptizing all people, teaching the flock, redressing sins, bringing people to salvation. A privatized church, no matter how extensively tolerated, is unable to live up to the potentiality of its energies that this kind of mission prescribes. With its energies curbed, the church finds itself a signatory of the social pact made for other interest groups. The French sociologist of religion, Emile Poulat, sees in the church's attitude as it emerges in our "post-Christian" times a universalization of Christianity through a gradual accommodation with modernity. This may be so, yet the tension also becomes manifest between the church's original message and those who are uncomfortable with practices

12. *Catholic Eye*, Nov. 1987.

adjusted to the requirements of civil society and its pluralism. Hence the surfacing of sects, old esoteric teachings, and the sciences of the occult. Poulat mentions that certain countries in the Latin world are "deeply de-christianized" while they have remained "tenaciously Catholic." Can these phenomena be listed as religious in the Catholic sense, or are they symptoms of a religious syncretism which puts out a welcoming mat to all? If mere curiosity or some vague "inner voice" claims the status of genuine faith, then the Roman Empire in its fifth-century decline was among the most religious environments: dozens of oriental, pagan, and other salvation-bringing sects (not to mention the mushrooming philosophical movements) were competing in a "pluralist" climate, with gurus and fakirs impressing their credulous public. Poulat concludes that, in view of his own area of study, there is no longer a specifically religious field to consider.

Thus, indicators focus on a new kind of *ecumenism.* Counter-churches arise not in the credal and institutional sense, but often as centers of attraction which pull Catholics away from the doctrinal and ethical manifestations of their church, and offer them a comfortable and seemingly normal substitute—pluralism, choice based on religious indifference. Weakened institutions, like lonely individuals, seek out the company of others. The contrast is remarkable between earlier phases of the church—with its sharp demarcation from other creeds and its triumphantly held certitudes—and the contemporary church's attempts at dialogue, common worship and causes, and concessions to ideological groups previously identified as heresies, unorthodoxies, sects too changeable and fickle, intrinsically perverse, not fit for even a temporary co-operation. Not only are the church's sharp edges now rounded; concessions are made in confusion and embarrassed silence, and practices are implemented that were anathematized only a few decades ago.

An entirely new situation arises: the core belief of the church is increasingly difficult to identify. Theoretically we know that Rome speaks with one voice; in essence, this has not changed. Yet, profiting by the surrounding climate of pluralism groups of Catholics raise their dissenting voices on all issues and occasions, and claim equal right to speak in the name of the church. In the Babel din, authority is not so much opposed as it is ignored; for the outside observer, the genuine sound of Catholic teaching is garbled, as if by the interference of hostile radio stations.

In the ensuing extraordinary confusion, *ecumenism*—since this is the label under which the church's new strategy is best known—is a method of inviting the ex-believers, half-believers, as well as the ecumenical partners themselves, to help the church amplify its religious orientation. While the religious message is, strictly speaking, unaltered, the message that ecumenism itself carries in reality deemphasizes the importance of the core teaching and reorientates it toward something more plausible than Catholicism, more suitable for the contemporary, pluralistic climate of opinion. The pretexts are at hand, supplied by the ideology of pluralism, and the ecumenical discourse runs along the following lines: Mankind is now groping towards unity, the end of sectarianism and other kinds of separation. This is a secular movement, but since the objective itself can only be secured through peace and tolerant understanding, the efforts are stamped by divine design and will. Religions and churches must take the lead in this project in order to overcome the still strong remnants of materialism, mistrust, and hostility. Whether at the United Nations (through the papal visits there) or in democratic-pluralistic societies, the ecumenical tendency should be promoted in spite of all the hurdles to cooperation, until the spiritual power of religion removes them and builds a peaceful world.

It is difficult to assess whether this discourse and the actions it inspires—for example, the planetary prayer meeting held in Assisi in October 1986 and repeated in Japan the following year—are the consequence of a change of Roman thinking in religious matters or a politically motivated strategy to refurbish Roman "triumphalism" and the church's reputation as the sole fortress of certitudes. In our age of confusion, the manipulators often fall victim to their own manipulation, and under the hammer blows of self-generated publicity they come to believe what was originally meant to appease the zeitgeist. But whether belief or political sloganeering, the ecumenical broadsides lend themselves to a disturbing interpretation. Influenced by the ways and means of liberal society, the church makes some of the current techniques its own: advertisement and the language of world unity, but above all the search for plausibility before the contemporary public opinion and those who shape it, principally the media.

Other religions see these efforts as pathetic signs of the church's weakness. Hinduism, Islam, and Judaism seek no dialogue with Rome and shun involvement in mundane events which would discredit them in the eyes of their own faithful.[13] Or they use the Roman eagerness for contacts and dialogue as a way of obtaining concessions, not on spiritual matters where dialogue is pointless (since all religions have their sui generis theology), but on political issues. In such cases they regard the church as a kind of Western leader sharing in Western decline, speaking not for Christ, which does not interest them anyway, but for a civilization on which they have long-standing claims.

The consequence of this ungenuine, surface ecumenism is an increase of spiritual confusion, as if the goal were a "united religions" on the pattern of the United Nations. This is all the easier thanks to the "opening of windows" that together with ecumenism has resulted in Roman eagerness to associate with heterodox organizations. What may appear as a generous call for cooperation becomes an acceptance of interference by the outside world. It takes the form of pressure groups acting, officially or not, inside a church that is eager to adopt the

13. When John Paul II visited India in 1985, huge protest efforts tried to cancel or obstruct the occasion. In a ceremony, the pope received a sign which symbolically turned him into a worshiper of Vishnu. Throughout the visit Hinduism was subtly extolled, at the expense of Christianity, to such an extent that Indian Catholics were embarrassed by the lack of resistance on the part of India's Catholic hierarchy. Islam's little regard for Christianity (Jesus was the last prophet of the Abrahamic line, before the greatest of all came, Allah's messenger Mohammed) is well known, no churches being allowed in *Dar es-Islam* ("the Gate of Islam," a term for Moslem territory). Jewish contact with Rome focuses on a distinct political objective, the recognition of the state of Israel by the Vatican.

fashionable public-relations gimmick of transparency. Thus dissenting churchmen, backed by these pressure groups, can now propose what is incompatible and adversarial to the church's teaching, but representative of the spirit of worldly pluralism. In so acting, the dissidents and acerbic critics are encouraged by powerful agencies of civil society and of the partners in ecumenism. There is hardly any danger for them: society offers its shelter. It consists of protection by the media: exposure of person and position to the limelight through a one-sided and favored orchestration. A challenger of orthodoxy is automatically guaranteed public appearances, prominence on the lecture circuit, invitations to publish, and a bestseller status for his ideas. The modern media are in essence chasing after sensations and they reward indiscriminately those with obvious publicity potential. Yet the media do make choices and instinctively favor not the orthodox who wants to unite the faithful, but the rebel who divides and fragments.

In the ongoing battle of state, civil society, and church, society's dominant position has given it—as always in the case of power elites—the monopoly on *interpretation*, the definition of vocabulary and meaning. It includes the formulation of concepts, the unquestionability of slogans, the verbal setting of objectives. It also includes the prevalence of a certain style, whether of speech, art, behavior, or dressing. Rebels against institutions, which possess their own style, concepts, objectives, and ways of dressing and behavior, adopt the behavior and ideas of power elites who encourage their rebellion and offer them a protective shelter. Today we see the challengers of ecclesiastical authority change into civil society's fashionable uniform—jeans and pullover, or business suit and tie—so as outwardly to signify their modification of loyalty. It is instructive to observe that the pope and his immediate entourage wear cassocks, while the wider ecclesiastical communities discard them except for certain occasions of striking a challenging stance for public shock value. In such instances, the respect that church attire still calls forth visibly clashes with the heterodox ideas expressed by its wearer. This is the intended impression, and the result is, indeed, a preprogrammed confusion, clash, and scandal. The cause of fragmentation chalks up another victory.

Several cases are so well known that the names attached to them have become watchwords, whether of political or sexual liberation. The names of the main challengers have acquired the weight of heroes in epic poems. Whose heroes? Those of civil society, which desires to become a "church." Meanwhile, men like Hans Küng, Leonardo Boff, Charles Curran, and others are surrounded by a potential microchurch, the model for which is available in the "base-communities." The parish and the diocese obviously cannot contain the challenger's ambition and scope; only new structures may correspond to new theologies. The question is not whether these microchurches will develop, gather strength, and endure; what is important from society's perspective is that they present one, two, or many alternative churches, eventually local and ephemeral coagulations of the church reduced to interest-group status, and so to plurality.

The objective is a classical one: to have the church serve society's policy and purpose. To many of our contemporaries this seems a reasonable objective, just as it seemed reasonable a few hundred years ago to loyal partisans of kings and emperors that the church should espouse the monarch's cause.

CHAPTER THREE

Gains or Losses?

A vast institution like the Catholic church—vast in time, space, and effect—does not display certifiable signs of alteration as readily as do smaller, more easily influenced institutions and communities. The Western world has known only one other institution, the Roman state (republic and empire), that has been similarly difficult to diagnose at any one time. When was it a healthy organism having imaginary or passing troubles, and when was it a structure on the way to decadence and decline? The many manifestations of troubles in the church already discussed may be, after all, of a temporary, and in the long run, superficial character. Enlarged within this century's perspective, within a few decades they may take on truer proportions. However, to every century its own perspective, its own self-evaluation. The symptoms discussed here appear to the limited wisdom of contemporaries—to millions of them, including clerics—as those of a great crisis. What are the church's options for survival in this age without losing its vital core—its faith—during this never-yet-seen process of adaptation to the world?

The question as we put it cannot be answered by the size of membership lists of parishes or other Catholic organizations like universities. Nor can the question about the continued impressiveness of the Vatican's display during solemn ceremonies. These external signs are still by and large the traditional ones, with a still imperial-style splendor about them—with the consequence that, statistically speaking, a large majority of

Catholics in the world may not be aware of the crisis, just as the masses in the Roman empire (some forty-five million inhabitants at the imperial apogee in the first centuries after Christ) were not aware of Rome's high point or decadence. But although from the point of view of religion the peace and salvation of souls are the essential questions, for those who meditate on the general state of Roman Catholicism as the church nears the year 2000, all the related issues possess a correspondingly crucial weight, particularly since for these individuals it is precisely the peace and salvation of souls that are at stake if the church emits messages of uncertainty, hesitation, or contradiction.

In short, it is not enough to worship and exalt God and dismiss this issue as settled; nor can we deny the value of ecclesiastical institutions here on earth, as if the right order of the soul could accommodate itself to organizational anarchy, dissolution, and mindless changes.[1] There is a call for permanence in human affairs also, lest the soul's equilibrium be endangered: the ecclesiastical corporation runs the risk of dislocation and dispersion along the lines of subjective individualism. The temptation of over-zealous people concerned only with heavenly matters, whom Mgr. Ronald Knox used to call "ultra-supernaturalists,"[2] is to exalt God in such a way as to atone for being merely human, for being in a natural need of institutions and guidelines. Let us not despise the human and thus the social order for not sharing entirely in the supernatural order.

The present crisis of the church is not more than a quarter century old, but the speed and direction of movement away from standards and tradition—in doctrine, faith, and practice—suggest an irreversible trend. The often violent or else camouflaged thrust away from the center is not in doubt, so

1. Let us keep in mind that the fundamental statements on which Western political thought rests were made by Plato. What pertains here may be read in several of the Platonic dialogues: the integrity of the political community depends on the right ordering of the citizen's soul. Hence the importance of education, the moral guidance of the young, the cultivation of philosophy.

2. See my book *Theists and Atheists: A Typology of Non-Belief* (The Hague: Mouton Publishers, 1980), particularly chapter 5, "God beyond God: The Ultra-Supernaturalist Search."

that we stand on plausible ground as we examine the choices available *now,* rather than the likelihood of an illusory "restoration." Of the church's evolving forms we can have no precise notion; we can, with our present knowledge, scrutinize the probabilities.

The Politics of Engagement

Numerous agents in the submission of the church to civil society have already been mentioned. But what has additionally facilitated this submission, the zeal and indecent ardor with which the church too has accepted civil society's injunctions and slogans, is the church's own *politization.* This is not a new thing; centuries ago prelates defended the divine right of kings, and were not inhibited in this endeavor even when the monarchy was waging war on the church. Today, many prelates and theologians are similarly indignant when the now dominant political form, democracy, comes under attack.[3] In other words, much of the accumulated capital of spirituality was then and is now misused for the purpose of gaining influence and status in the political world, for being present in every major movement, for flattering the powerful, and finally, for being accepted by them. To be sure, the general reason for this attitude is this: the twentieth-century church does not want to suffer further losses after two centuries of a poor record—the desertion of the Voltairean (liberal, business- and pleasure-centered) bourgeoisie, and the Marxian (organized, revendicatory, revolutionary) proletariat. Considering that the new overwhelmingly anticlerical and agnostic society has been organized and permeated by liberal ideology on the model of pluralism and wholesale participation, churchmen felt that the times no longer favor a church which depends on traditional classes, but that the church must be everywhere present in the

3. Attacking the Vatican *Instruction* of 1987 against biogenetic manipulation, P. Ladrière, editor of the critical volume *Le retour des certitudes,* calls the document contrary to democracy (!) because it instructs citizens protected by the laws of separation of church and state. Quoted in "Les origines d'un dépit," *Catholica* 6 (February 1988): 4-6.

modern classless society. It should therefore loosen its structure and modernize its discourse according to the democratic
model and delegate its representatives to those mass movements and pressure groups which seem in the forefront of
organizing the future.[4]

Such a dispersion of interest and involvement (*engage-
ment,* to use the fashionable, Sartrian term) carried various
dangers. The ecclesiastics so delegated, and increasingly self-
delegated, to every corner of civil society were not always
intelligent and subtle diplomats, as was true when society,
more unified (less pluralist) and governed by the state, needed
only a few brilliant and devoted churchmen to secure the
Roman influence at high places. The consequence of too many
involved ecclesiastics was a weakened influence; many of
Rome's representatives fell under the influence of the very
milieu they had been called upon to Christianize, or, as the case
may be, to keep on the confessional track. A reverse operation,
a counterproductive movement, appeared; instead of bringing
syndicalists, students, journalists, artists, businessmen, and
professors to the faith, or detaching them from freemasonry,
Marxism, atheism, and, lately, oriental sects, these groups,
with civil society's ideological backing, exerted *their* own attraction on priests, theologians, members of Catholic universities and media, and finally on bishops and diocesan personnel.
It is no exaggeration to say that the lines of thought proposed
by such church-sponsored organizations as the Catholic Action, mostly in the interwar period, or those like the worker-
priests, opposed by the Vatican in the 1950s, found their way
into a number of important conciliar documents. Or, if these
documents did not contain the essential messages of the Council, they were heralded as such by the combined lay and

4. The most cogent critique of this approach to the Christian apostolate
has come from the pen of Islamologist Henry Corbin. (See his *Le paradoxe du
monothéisme* [Paris: Editions de l'Herne, 1981].) Corbin's thesis, embracing the
entire Christian past, is that it is inherent to Christian monotheism that God
(and so theology and sacred history) is brought to bear, without any mediation,
on all aspects of life: politics, social movements, science, etc. At the end,
religion suffers the same ills that trouble society: it is unable to extricate itself
from the decline of society.

ecclesiastical groups which, called by then the church's avant-garde on intellectual and social matters, could play a decisive role before, during, and after Vatican II. This explains an increasing number of sermons, homilies, and episcopal letters no longer directed at the care of souls and the explanation of doctrine, but serving rather as occasions for comments on political issues (inevitably colored by partisanship) such as "democratization," "the rehabilitation of Martin Luther," the "humanization of religion and Jesus Christ," the "updating of moral teaching," and even the "cause of the people of God against the Church's hierarchy."[5]

In hundreds of churches every Sunday, or on weekdays in church-sponsored gatherings and catechetical classes, an indifferent or outright opposition discourse is amplified and grows. From pulpit and press, communities of believers are exposed to propaganda sermons of "social justice" (seen from a "progressive" angle), "human rights," and disobedience to superiors—without a word about life in communion with God, the necessity to pray, or the obligation to keep the moral law, to go to the sacraments, to be surrounded by consecrated beauty, itself a source of deepened Christian life. On the contrary, each time civil society proposes a new fad, from sex education to pacifism, it mobilizes ecclesiastics—initiating controversy, splitting opinion, appealing to passions. As soon as a politicized issue (for example, feminism) appears on the screen of civil society, priests and nuns, theologians and bishops rush to dogmatize its program and make their continued loyalty to the church conditional on whether Rome is willing to shed its "sexist" and "male-chauvinist" attitude. And so on and on, with an endless number of issues.

With these cases and examples all too well known to the average Catholic parishioner or newspaper reader, I wish to illustrate two things. First, the church's effort not to lose new categories of people according to the pattern of the last two centuries seems a failure of vast dimensions. What the church

5. It is understood that I omit here the "juicier" topics like the homosexuality of Jesus or the acceptability of alternative lifestyles including such practices as masturbation, sodomy, or incest.

has gained is its presence in newsrooms, television studios, and international bodies, but not always through its best spokesmen. Most often these spokesmen have *not* been representatives of the "other kingdom," but somewhat alien-tongued agents of civil society itself, credited with making estimable, though still awkward, efforts to conform to civil society, our common mother.

Second, the post-Vatican church has in this way put itself in an irreversible situation of politization. What has been added to religious life is not more soul, nor more charity (ecclesiastical bureaucracy is colder and more impersonal than ever), but only more aptitude for propaganda and sloganeering. What has happened in the past twenty-five years is not the usual acceptance, on the church's part, of newly emerged shapes of the world, a world always to be criticized, corrected, and converted, but instead a deeply penetrating secularization of the church itself. In sum, a situation of losers: civil society drowned in the pride of its self-sufficiency, and a subservient church refusing to convert this drunken giant.

Option A

What then are the choices facing Rome today? We see two options that the church may take, options modelled on the state of the modern world. *Option A* is the course of accommodation with pluralistic and liberal democracy; *Option B* is accommodation with socialism and the Left.[6]

Option A. In times of persecution and distress throughout history certain thinkers in the church have remembered the first experiences in pagan Rome. If those lessons are still valid, they suggest a large degree of external accommodation and a

6. The church had other options in the past. The one that Emperor Constantine offered in A.D. 313, acceptance as a free, then as a state, religion, was a choice that was to lead to imperial responsibilities passed on from extinct Rome to the church for administrative tasks. Options at such levels have world-historical significance and resonance. Does the choice facing the church today carry a similar, history-making weight, or is it made under the pressure of various accommodation offers?

clandestine survival of the inner core of the faith. The *Letter to Diognetes,* an anonymous document apparently of the first half of the second century (ca. A.D. 130), addressed to a baptismal candidate, insisted that Christians were not only loyal citizens of the empire, but were indeed better than the pagans. Christ's teaching justifies the temporal power of the emperor, said the writer, as part of God's will. (This was also the view of Tertullian, the prominent church father.) The Christians, whether artisans or housewives, soldiers or teachers, fulfilled their daily tasks; they were generally better citizens than the pagans, abstaining from crime, violence, and immoral acts. Another list of loyal behavior could be drawn up today—John Courtney Murray has suggested one by emphasizing the thorough compatibility of citizenship in the American democracy with fidelity to the church.

What the author of the *Letter to Diognetes* and subsequent readers could not forget was the recurrent persecution of Christians. It did not dampen their acceptance of the task of citizenship, but it certainly sharpened their awareness of the difference between the two kingdoms, that of God and that of men. The difference was brought home to them on the ten major occasions of Roman persecution, from the first under Nero in the first century A.D. to the last under Diocletian and his successors, more than two centuries later; but it was also brought home, at least to the Christian elite, by the Platonic teaching that man lives in two worlds: one of ideas, the other of their copies; one of perfection and necessity, the other of the contingent and imperfect. This universal teaching and experience seems to have been erased from the mind of modern man. For him there is only one world, the human world of ordinary ambitions and disappointments, generally neutral, meaningless, and punctuated by "events" whose incidence is muted by a battery of collective safeguards and therapeutic measures. In this situation the great majority of Catholics feel that everything is in order and that they are not called upon by society to sacrifice to the "emperor." Yet in the last two decades, Western legislatures have passed laws which clash head-on with Christian moral law. Christians in Rome regarded such laws as a provocation, and resisted them to the death. In contrast, statistical figures indicate that today's "updated" Catholic, like his fellow citizens of other faiths, readily admits that agencies of government and civil society circumscribe his moral existence from cradle to grave, but he admits that the church may less and less dictate his moral conduct against his own opinions and convenience. This situation is a complete reversal from that of the early Christians in imperial Rome.

In other words, a wide area of incompatibility remains between citizenship and faith (between the "two kingdoms"); the Christian citizen has only changed masters in things moral and behavioral, although he believes it when he is told that he is *now* free of such a control. He is not aware that, as matters stand, both the laws and the public mores keep him corralled within narrow limits, so that his freedom of choice is not wider than was that of the recipient of the *Letter to Diognetes*. In fact, the contemporary Diognetes is supposed to consider the new limitations as actually "liberating": large-scale abortions, experiments with the aborted fetus, school instruction on homosexual lifestyle, and so on. These immoral laws, in some respects not different from those prevailing in pagan Roman society, are today part of the social environment and the values of contemporary culture.[7]

One would have supposed that, confronted with this increasing incompatibility between liberal democratic society and itself, the church would hasten to offer an alternative milieu filled with its own teaching and values. However, it seems that the church lacks inspiration and will to constitute a social environment and originate independent cultural values from its vast reserves. After all, are Catholic universities different from others? Is less vulgar television watched in seminaries than at lay fraternity houses? Hardly anything may be found as contradicting the uni-dimensionality of the average

7. Fr. Francis Canavan has now located the "ultimate liberation," namely masturbation as safe sex in a world of AIDS. He writes regarding a book by Betty Dodson, *Sex for One* (see *Catholic Eye,* 17 March 1988) that this reduction of sex to masturbation is the logical outcome of the "autonomous individual of liberal theory," one who is the sole source of judgments, will, and appetites.

Catholic's moral existence. He could subscribe without great pangs of conscience to what John Dewey advocated in his book, *A Common Faith* (1934): "Here are all the elements for a religious faith that shall not be confined to sect, class, or race. Such a faith has always been implicitly the common faith of mankind. It remains to make it explicit and militant."[8]

Note Dewey's tranquil confidence that these are indeed incontrovertibly true dogmas, and compare this confidence with the anxious, quick denials by so many Catholic public figures that they might hold views opposed to the accepted public philosophy.[9] A comparison between secular humanist Dewey's clear affirmation and the elusive gesture of Catholic public figures indicates the direction of a substantial, perhaps commanding, segment of the church. In an age when "authority" is an avoided term, and its practice severely condemned, the tendency of church leaders is to subscribe to the popular view. Sociologically, this choice points to what liberal-pluralist democracy offers—just what pagan emperor worship offered 2000 years ago—a comfortable coexistence between one's conscience and the prevailing political-legal forms, whatever they may be. Christians in Roman society were sorely tempted to perform the few gestures before the magistrate and the imperial effigy in order to avoid arrest and persecution. However, a majority must have resisted capitulation to the judge and the officials, and most often the bishops were in the frontline of the resistance. With rare exceptions, today's bishops follow the easy course and recommend conformity not only to laws,

8. Here are the articles of this new faith as listed a year before (1933) as the *Humanist Manifesto*, prepared by Dewey and his collaborators. (1) The universe is self-existing, not created; (2) science shows the unreality of supernatural sanctions for human values; (3) earthly existence is the beginning and end for any individual; (4) religious emotions are best expressed in heightened individuals and in efforts to advance social well-being; (5) man himself is maker and active power, unmoved by transcendent forces.

9. Many churchmen not wishing to adhere to Marxism opt for initiation to or alliance with freemasonry, which has far-reaching power and influence, particularly among the elite of society. Their political influence is strong in lawmaking, such as abortion laws. Alliance with freemasonry is forbidden by the church.

whatever they may be in their blatant contradiction of the moral law, but also to the latest twist and turn of public attitude.

Thus Option A is but a way of swimming with the current, dictated by public opinion and its pressure groups. Less than three decades after the Vatican Council, the church in its comfortable corner is temporarily tolerated even by the militants of Deweyite humanism, because they and other secularists have understood, like Lenin in his time, that one can do the job of weakening the church's influence better by entrusting the task to the church itself. Suicide looks better than murder. Finding its niche in civil society, the church supplies the alibi needed to confirm this toleration. Down the present path, the church's future may be projected by the following snapshots: still a vast institution, still a place of solemnities and ceremonies, the church may become eclectic enough to admit alien "cultural" elements into its ritual; or the church may become a sheltered institution, resembling a venerable academy where research is pursued in a busy bureaucratic setting, and where social work is also performed as a kind of repayment to society for the leisure it secures; or it may become a nucleus of worshipers, their faith expressed in a no-longer comprehended, quasi-esoteric language and liturgy which permit references to a historical justification of (rather, antiquarian interest in) the church's existence and its founder.

Let us face the fact—Option A for the church is the acceptance of marginalization, a slow glide down to irrelevance and finally decline. The church may no longer count on a mostly favorable milieu, a secure sociocultural environment. It has no solid institutional partnerships; the political realm has become indifferent or hostile, and civil society has been constructed in precise opposition to the doctrinal content of the church and its concept of authority. If in the past critics could speak of a church exaggeratedly involved with the higher levels of political power, we may now speak of a "socialized" *ecclesia* seeking new alliances with the new power elites of civil society. The plain truth is, not only the Catholic church, but Christianity as such has ceased to be the dynamic carrier of civilizational quests. It does not fire modern man's imagination, it is not associated to his dreams. Leszek Kolakowski, the ex-Marxist philosopher, made these two points in an interview with the Yugoslav writer, Mihajlov: "First, it is very unlikely that the discovery of the absolute could occur outside of humanity's religious tradition. Second, it is not only in communist countries, but also in the industrialized nations of the West that people, particularly young people, evince all manner of symptoms of alarm and a powerful urge to seek something else, something that our present civilization is unable to provide."[10]

This is the time when the church has, at least in practice, if not always officially, abolished the aesthetic component in its liturgy, language, and sacramental life, thereby confusing worshipers and inciting them to seek pseudo-satisfaction in the faddist forms of contemporary culture. Writing about church music, Cardinal Ratzinger notes that in the new culture music "has received the function of arousing irrational powers," shaping a new consciousness. Reflecting on the role of this music in the liturgy, Ratzinger observes that it prompts a new solidarity in communities "supposed to bring forth a new people of God, although God here really means the people themselves and the historical energies realized in them."[11] A well-chosen illustration which also complements Kolakowski's words. Music, together with architecture, is always a good indicator of the spirit of the age, and now it serves a "revolutionary arousal," thus forming a new consciousness and conquering vast segments of Christians. The genuine response to youth seeking "something else than what our present situation offers" is not a church music with revolutionary arousal, but a return to Palestrina, Bach, and Couperin. Similarly, the answer to the sexual excitement on which our civilization avidly insists is not sex education and the safe way of using condoms, but a relearning of asceticism, morally vindicated, if ever, in the present circumstances.

The logical outcome of Option A presented here is not a

10. *The New Leader,* 7 Sept. 1987.

11. "Liturgy and Church Music," in *Homiletic and Pastoral Review* (June 1986).

new thesis, but was in the back of every serious analysis of the decadence phenomenon, no matter when and where it occurred. It was put in a striking formula by Max Weber, who spoke of the "bureaucratization of charisma," a vivid manner of expressing what we witness around us today. It is not a question of distributing blame. All of a sudden the weight of history seems to descend on a vast organization like heavy grey clouds on a sunny landscape. The colorful meadows, woods, fields, and flowers lose their playful liveliness, and those who walked through the area picking flowers, grabbing Mother Earth with avid fingers, carving names on the trees, now appear tired, listless, and uncaring. In Weber's words, and speaking of institutions or empires, "bureaucratization" sets in; others call it ossification, reification, a hardening of the arteries, and other such terms usually borrowed from biology or psychology. For our purpose, Cicero's remark sums it up when he notes that the Roman priests in charge of performing sacrifice smiled like accomplices on passing each other. They knew they belonged to a well-remunerated sacerdotal *collegium*, but they also knew that their sacralized gestures had become empty. No wonder that Middle Eastern belief systems were able to flood such a vacuum, dislodging the lost religious meaning.

Spokesmen for Accommodation

Before it became an anxiety-filled naked obligation to choose, Option A was a label for learned treatises by outstanding Catholic scholars of this century who, before the coup d'état of Vatican II, were exploring *options*. These explorations did not amount to policy decisions made in times of certitude in response to the world's rich appeals to its recognized moral authority. The explorations aimed rather at preparing the church for hard times of increasing secularization in the cultural milieu. The prevailing trend was accommodationist, with the questions being only whether any partners for dialogue would remain, and accommodation at what level. Roughly three categories of scholars engaged in ascertaining the ripeness of the times *(kairos)*, when in reality they were weighing the future beyond the crisis and the possibilities that the time of crisis might allow.

Briefly put, one school sought a historical accord with leftist mass movements, seen as the main line of history's future course. The ancestor here had been the abbé Lamennais (in the 1820s and 1830s), whose fervent recommendation to the papacy was to choose, while it could, the working class as its partner against the monarchy (defeated by the Revolution), and against the then triumphing bourgeoisie. Lamennais' prophecy was that, in turn, the bourgeoisie too would go under (besides, its liberal ideology contradicted Christ's teaching) and the proletariat would then become the history-making force, carrying a truer message. This thesis, when updated a century later, found other spokesmen: priests like Chenu, Montuclard, Congar, and for a time Jacques Maritain. All believed that the Marxist parties would bypass the church's sloweddown evangelization, and that this was a positive development since the poor must first be given bread, and afterwards the faith. The worker-priest movement was a product of these convictions, and its predictable consequence was twofold: rejection by Rome (Pius XII) and the priests' detachment from ministry in favor of an exclusively communist or syndicalist militancy.

The prominent representative of the second school of thought is Karl Rahner, who was not involved in the revolutionary tradition of his French fellow theologians. Rahner did not see the crisis as a social-economic phenomenon, but as a crisis of faith. In the modern, scientific, and intellectually sophisticated world, the faith, as presented by the church, is no longer acceptable to the dominant category of cultured urban critics.[12] They could be reached, Rahner believed, as

12. Karl Rahner's experience in postwar Germany focused on the drifting intelligentsia, marked by repentance for Hitler's crimes and giving credence to the propaganda that the church was the Nazi regime's silent accomplice. Unlike their French colleagues, these intellectuals were not, at least in large numbers, attracted to Marxism, which was too visible in ruling Germany's other half. Yet they felt compelled to renounce the prewar ideals of faith and nationhood.

"anonymous Christians" whose existential ground is affected by God's "self-communication." Each may react in his intimate subjective self, but for this to happen the church must first deemphasize the objective content of the faith and make God accessible through the categories of subjectivism. God is relocated to the depth of the self so that we encounter him at the intersection of our most intimate experience with the world. The act of faith becomes expendable because man's essence and God's essence are the same.[13]

The third school of thought, the most influential before the Council (thanks to papal sponsorship)[14] was represented by Jacques Maritain. We might say that Option A was his brainchild. Maritain was born in the nineteenth century as a Protestant and remained permeated by that century's liberal thought in which many prominent minds, Protestant and Catholic alike, came together, so that even after his conversion Maritain had no trouble further elaborating his Christian-liberal synthesis.[15] Briefly put, this synthesis accepts the common good as defined by democratic society—in Maritain's view the heiress of the gospels!—without any addition by religious thought (in *Human Rights and Natural Law*). It favorably registers the fact that Christians may live at peace with their religion in such a society. We note here a significant difference from earlier nineteenth-century lay Catholic thinking, that of Chateaubriand, Tocqueville, or Lord Acton. At the threshold of the democratic age they expressed the hope that Catholicism, by which they understood the church's doctrinal stand and the moral and cultural consequences following from it, would remain a preponderantly active element in the new society;

13. It is obvious even from this short summary that Rahner's chief inspiration is derived from Heidegger and Rudolf Bultmann.

14. As the objective affirmations of faith and doctrine weaken, the personal philosophies and discipleships of the popes are pushed into the foreground. Pius XII was still a strict Thomist, but Paul VI was an admiring disciple of Jacques Maritain, while John Paul II had his intellectual formation under the masters of phenomenology and personalism, mainly Max Scheler.

15. After about a fifteen-year period, during which the fresh convert elaborated right-wing ideas: for example, in *Three Reformers*, a critique of Luther, Descartes, and Rousseau.

otherwise society would risk being pulled apart by subjective and factional forces, according to the individualistic inspiration of liberalism and relativism. They argued that authority—and in a democracy this would be not political but religious—must remain central to society as a counterweight to centrifugal tendencies in the initial period, and to the ensuing totalitarian thrust to follow.[16]

Maritain saw it differently. During the years of the Second World War that he spent teaching at universities in the United States (Chicago, Notre Dame, Princeton), he formulated an equation between the democratic regime and a church no longer shouldering historical responsibilities that best approximated the Christian form of life a political community could adopt. Thus in the 1940s and early 1950s he thought that a modern democratic regime may offer a sufficient guarantee for the semi-public and certainly the private practice of the Christian religion. More than this was unnecessary since the basic inspiration of democracy was anyway Christian—a conclusion in which we see Maritain's return to his Protestant background. This is not the place to discuss Maritain's views (on "integral humanism," for example). Suffice it to say that in the already mentioned *Three Reformers* (1925) he had harshly criticized Luther, Descartes, and Rousseau precisely for introducing democratic ideas into philosophical and religious discourse, and so into the area of politics.

The three categories examined through their typical representatives, Chenu, Rahner, and Maritain,[17] are united in proposing some form of accommodation with the world and worldly philosophies: the socialist Left, democratic liberalism,

16. Let us note that this relative optimism with regard to liberal-pluralistic democracy was not shared by Pius IX and Pius X.

17. The thought of Teilhard de Chardin represents here an even more radical departure from traditional Catholic doctrine, although in retrospect he seems more typical of the modern deviation. Teilhard admitted he wanted "to graft a new shoot on the old Roman stem," entirely in accord with a self-formulated evolutionary theory in which super-mankind and the super-Christ arrive, the first conditioning the second, at Point Omega. Teilhard's phantasms appeal as strongly to contemporary sensibilities as Rahner's subjectivism or Maritain's sacralized democracy.

and fashionable systems like existentialism and pantheism. They take it implicitly for granted[18] that the Roman worldview is too exhausted to inspire new modes of thought and action, and that therefore Catholicism—its politics, culture, and involvement in the world—can do nothing better than remain somewhat inertly present, trying at best occasionally to nuance the mundane attitudes in their radical excesses. To be sure, this is not a uniform policy: acquiescence alternates with critique and with the reaffirmation of doctrinal points which oppose the trend. As illustrations, I referred to the encyclical *Humanae Vitae* (1968), and to the *Instruction* (1987) against biogenetic manipulations. We may also add Mgr. Ratzinger's attacks on millenarist-utopian ideology, and the *Monitum* (1962) directed against the highly unorthodox hypotheses of Teilhard de Chardin, who wanted "to graft the shoot of evolutionism on the old Roman stem," but who succeeded only in fantasizing about a "super-Christ" rising with the maturation of a "super-mankind" at Point Omega.

But overall the contemporary church intends to hitch its carriage to the world's locomotives. Modern ideology, with its ambition fired by notorious achievements—technology, health care, mastery over some chronic social ills—is convinced that mankind has reached a satisfying end station and that it now possesses the means of settling the few remaining details. In fine, everything seems to be a matter for technology (social engineering, psychotechniques, psychopedagogy, etc.) to bear on points where man's spontaneous insight is judged insufficient or where persuasion by science has so far been hindered.

While the church never doctrinally or officially subscribes to this overconfidence, throughout the centuries it has so often witnessed the overbearing but ephemeral self-praise of generations that it is now unable to point to its groundless-

18. Karl Rahner died only a few years ago; his epigones have had no time to nuance his thought. But Henri de Lubac recognized long ago his modernist errors, and Maritain's last book, *The Peasant of the Garonne,* mocks the modernists, among them Teilhard. The book amounts to a partial self-criticism.

ness. In the absence of reaffirmed truth, doctrinally *and* culturally, many Catholics become dazzled by the novelties and follow society's ideological lead. Besieged from outside and inside by clamors of ultimate wisdom, Rome hopes to pass unnoticed, as it were, and not call attention to its own alleged "stagnation," "outmoded dogmatism," "sexism," and other "obstinacies."

Cardinal Ratzinger tackles, perhaps unwittingly, the issue of Option A in his *Report* when he addresses the problem of liberation theology. On the surface, he discusses the condition of ordinary parishes and Catholic groups, and mentions that what used to be the *sensus fidei* and the magisterium—that is, the process of the formulation of the faith—is now perceived as the community's understanding and interpretation of Scripture. The Protestant impact is unmistakable: the community interprets the events on the basis of its experience, and thus discovers what its practice should be. The question arises: Is what Ratzinger describes not also a kind of "liberation theology"? It is increasingly difficult to distinguish between, for example, what groups of South American clergy and episcopate preach as a theology of liberation, more or less unified under the double Marxist-Christian banner, and the various theologies taught in many places outside South America in dioceses, seminaries, universities, and Catholic publications. In other words, liberation theology now enjoys an unspoken authorization to teach heterodoxy and to put what it teaches into practice. "Love and do what you will" used to be an unequivocal message, since the love of Christ was meant. But now "love" may mean the use of guns in a guerrilla war, sodomic acts, vulgar liturgies for fun, or abortion as a woman's right to her body.

The confusion in the ranks of the church has its parallel in inter-religious relations. "The impression has gained ground," Ratzinger notes apropos of the Catholic-Anglican dialogue on reunification, "of a kind of 'ecumenical dogma' in the process of emergence." We mentioned in a previous chapter that the vogue of ecumenism is a sign of the church's weakness, its belief that the liberal-pluralist tone of the age requires that thinking and action take the form of networks, permanent communication, and a fraternal sugarcoating. The desired end seems to be a blending in a higher, planetary unity. Unity in Christ is of course desirable, and over the ages some outstanding persons like Nicholas of Cusa, Bishop Bossuet, and the philosopher Leibniz have worked hard for it. In the present situation, however, the offers from the Vatican of an ecumenical dialogue must be read as signs of a feeling of inadequacy, as a diversionary move hiding deep internal uncertainties—as if backing from the world's religions can authenticate Rome's actions and as if the adoption of the current international formulas (United Nations, Unesco, Unicef, OAS, OAF, etc.) has the power to promote a "united religious organization." True, Ratzinger dismissed these efforts: "Jesus did not want to found a Catholic party within a cosmopolitan debating society."[19] And he added that the conclusion of ecumenical efforts was not in sight, since the differences have remained vigorous if one focuses on essentials. One more reason, then, to deplore the assembly in Assisi (October 12, 1986) for leaders of all beliefs to pray for world peace (from snake charmer American Indians to Taoist bonzes), repeated the following year at Kyoto, and then at Oxford. Are these gatherings, one may wonder, nonserious exercises in a superficial fraternization, or attempts at calling together a "constituent assembly" in view of drawing up a charter for the organization of a "united religions"?

Yet, ecumenism has another aspect too. It is not addressed to other churches alone, but is rather a mirror image and encouragement of pluralism within the church. The message that the ecumenical dialogue conveys to restless Catholics is that all opinions are invited to the platform, all conducts and lifestyles are equivalent. Extend this line of thought and you obtain a radical modification of the Roman structure in the direction of modern democracy: the platform, once people get used to it, is made permanent; it seats elected representatives,

---

19. Joseph Ratzinger, *Eglise, oecuménisme et politique* (Paris: Fayard, 1987), p. 125.

introduces regular consultation, and then the vote. A world religion may never come into existence—it would soon fall apart into sects—but the Roman doctrine and structure would be dismantled.

In spite of Cardinal Ratzinger's reassuring remarks rejecting the notion of a "cosmopolitan debating society," the connection seems at least to remain in the thinking of important Catholic hierarchs that (a) religious unity is a positive thing, and (b) Rome ought to consent to a lion's share of the concessions. In fact, in the last two decades Rome has given way to many demands that had for centuries clamored for admittance outside its walls. Option A thus means satisfaction given to a long list of heterodox claims laid against the church at one or another time by the notorious heresies, now combined in one offensive. Yves Congar's famous expression, "the October Revolution of the Church" (speaking of Vatican II) sums up the course of recent events: first, the structure is pried open by destructive forces which remain latent under anodine programs (before the Council, called "liturgical reforms" and "aggiornamento"). When authority's faith in itself begins to totter (John XXIII calls the Council), the adversary groups become aggressively reformist. Some of these groups turn into battering rams (pressure groups of bishops, coteries of theologians, and progressive journalists during and after the Council); manipulating the weapons of publicity, they create the impression of dominating events. The earlier majority of moderate bishops (as usual, a silent majority), intimidated by their own silence—hence, by feelings of isolation—becomes a headless conglomerate, and soon a persecuted minority.[20]

The implementation of the accommodationist program—the result of Option A—may be labeled a revolutionary program, but it is a latent one, working its way through the fabric of society (or of the church), converting institutions to its own

20. One group of bishops, including many from missionary areas, remained uncommitted to the "palace revolution." In their eyes, used to the sight of real human misery, the Council was debating matters irrelevant to their ministry.

cause.[21] Along the way any rebels against civil society are bought off. This is a feasible strategy, and one can say that it works for the interest of both society and its insurgents. The former has an accumulated capital through which it is able to finance the initial stages of the insurrection, not only with monetary bribes, but also and importantly with sociocultural participation. The rebels receive their subsidies in the shape of public forums that open for them (in media participation, at universities, and through foundation grants), so that they enter upon a kind of symbiosis with the society they plan to subvert and take over. Thus the revolution can spare its efforts of working its way through the masses—which used to be the classical procedure—and society is spared the shock of bombs and weapon-wielding terror. The result will be approximately the same, but only in the long run; a whole generation will be onlookers instead of victims.

Applied to the Roman church, the policy of post-conciliar accommodation copied from the methods of modern civil society penetrates through the new, postwar bourgeoisie, whose raison d'être and self-identification are no longer mainly economic but cultural. In this context "culture" means a lifestyle without other restraints than what fad and fashion dictate to this class of rootlessness and dismissed tradition; only the urges and whims of the moment matter, both in the routine of life and in worldview. This is the "hedonistic upper bourgeoisie of Europe and North America" to which Ratzinger referred in his *Report*, a new social class proud of having discarded religion and morals as well as any human limitations. In our egalitarian landscape this invisible or camouflaged elite sets the cultural tone. Its tastes and preferences are mirrored in the media, in magazines devoted to life's comforts and pleasures, and also in the curricula of schools. For business enterprises and intellectual and artistic movements to succeed, their merchandise and

---

21. This is what German sociologist Helmut Schelsky (died in 1984) called "the long march through the institutions," true especially of his own country which did not experience the outbreak of the "events" of May 1968 which toppled de Gaulle in neighboring France.

offerings must go through a subtle process of approval and assimilation by this class, which holds sway over the avenues of publicity, career, and political and intellectual prominence.

Now, like leading classes anywhere in history, the neo-hedonistic bourgeoisie focuses its efforts on power and cultural arbitration, one conditioning the other. The "old religion" has hardly any appeal for it; in reality, this class insists on having its own moral standards, and it can have them by pressuring the churches to promulgate new guidelines, rescinding the traditional ones and letting them fall into oblivion. A comparative and instructive study would show that around the year 1000—that is, before the emergence of some exceptionally strong popes, the rise of towns and of the influential mendicant orders—the nascent and muscular feudal society had similar ambitions: to impose its own mores and outlook on the church.[22] The difference was that the sacral character of feudal society depended on Christianity, its faith and dogmas, whereas the character of modern civil society is such that it can afford merely to tolerate the church, but not to integrate the supernatural claim in its own intellectual outlook. Thus the neo-bourgeoisie is able culturally to blackmail the church into effecting liturgical and doctrinal modifications, though its interest is only in lifting sexual and generally moral prohibitions. With some exaggeration one may say that it wishes to exercise a kind of *intellectual magisterium*, equidistant from last century's crude Voltairean or Darwinian disbelief and from traditional monotheism.

These hedonistic aspirations and neo-bourgeois ("yuppie") pressures do not justify, however, the church's own quasi-spontaneous desire to accommodate them, a desire which, after all, found expression three decades ago in the term "updating." While a Catholic bourgeoisie is new in the United States (its *prise de conscience* dates back only to the Kennedy

22. Even the most immoral, blaspheming, and whoring warlords wanted to build and endow churches, monasteries, and shrines so as to secure their peace of soul and salvation. This was a powerful weapon in ecclesiastical hands. See the brilliant work of Georges Duby, *William Marshal: The Flower of Chivalry* (New York: Pantheon Books, 1986).

presidency and Cardinal Spellman's global activities), it is very old in other parts of the world, in South America and Europe. Thus Rome ought to know how to deal with the "rebellion," except that it too is impressed by the "new age"; it too participated in the celebrations of the 1960s: one-worldism through decolonization; debunking of cult figures, whether Stalin or Pius XII; the promises of global democracy, postwar prosperity, and the calling of the Council itself. Church officials, blinded by the prospect of a planetary "new deal," responded to confused but persistent demands by their intellectuals for a democratic church tolerant of all opinion and behavior, for the rehabilitation of Luther and Galileo, for the establishment in retrospect of ecumenism.[23] There was no reason to call a halt at that point: Why should there be an "infallible magisterium" dictating to consciences, some American Catholics of the activist minority were asking, when in our country we only obey elected officials who change at regular intervals and have limited powers anyway? Why should theologians not be free, some members of this corporation asked, to set up their own magisterium, equivalent in authority to that of the church? Why should we, "people of God," follow "authorized" morality when the democratic age has discarded all taboos? And so, on and on, the challenge has been thrown at Rome about a married clergy, free divorce, licit masturbation, and fancy masses.

What these demands—always made by an aggressive minority, then vaguely echoed among the multitude and reverberating in the progressive media—suggest is, first, that the distinction of the "two kingdoms" has been fading in people's minds; and second, that Catholic intellectuals and theologians are aware of the weakening of Roman authority. The motive in both cases indicates that the ideologies of the models followed by society recognize no transcendence, or institutions which represent it, and know no authority save a pluralist structure.

---

23. In the pseudo-enthusiasm generated by the Council, Paulist Father P. Sheerin suggested to a gathering of Jews a change in the name of the Old Testament because "old" is an offensive term! Sheerin's interlocutors indignantly rejected this alleged good-will gesture, so typical of the 1960s.

Rome ought to have known how to deal with the situation, because the claims it had to confront were merely new versions of ancient protests against the Christian injunction to live in two worlds, the spiritual and the political. Many Catholics seemed to forget that this is precisely one of the chief glories of their religion—Christ's command about God and Caesar—and that actually the freedom of both, and of the citizen-worshiper, is thereby safeguarded. As the nineteenth-century Catholic thinkers wrote, since modern democracy was not structured the way traditional society had been it was in greater need of a spiritual authority—a shelter, among other things, from political majorities with their tyranny, and from the tutelary state inclined to despotism. In spite of these evidences—evidences unacceptable to liberal-pluralist civil society—the actors and spectators of the current drama do not grasp the fact that the church is not spiritually activated but rather paralyzed by the present situation.[24] In contrast to many other institutions, from the firehouse to orphanages, from business enterprises to sports clubs, the church alone has signed an invisible contract with civil society according to which it is obliged (a) to put restrictions on itself in opposition to its essential mission, and (b) to tolerate its own members, including the ecclesiastical personnel, becoming deserters to its rules and truth. It might be impossible to say how much of this self-restriction and tolerance of desertion is the product of civil society's influence and how much is a result of the church's vanishing authority. The fact is, there must be a correlation: the wider the church opens to civil society—its elites, its media, its values and culture—the less authority it

24. American conservatives claiming to be obedient Catholics regularly denounce papal encyclicals (e.g., *Sollicitudo Rei Socialis*, 1988) which criticize the spirit of capitalist economy. They forget the doctrinal and historical affinity of the church with corporatism—sometimes erroneously equated with socialism—and the church's refusal to endorse an individualistic system. This is one of the points of conflict between church and modern civil society, with its exclusively materialistic standards. Economic efficiency cannot be a central value in the church's social doctrine; full-scale capitalism, leaving solutions up to the forces of the market, contradicts the principle of subsidiarity which conservatives profess to hold in high esteem.

possesses and is able to exercise. It is a fatal, self-accelerating spiral.

What the Danish philosopher, Søren Kierkegaard, wrote 140 years ago about the secularization and bureaucratization of the Danish Lutheran Church—namely, its self-restriction, loss of authority, and ecclesiastical desertion—is strikingly apposite today. "The misfortune of our age . . . is disobedience, unwillingness to obey. And one deceives oneself and others by wishing to make us imagine that it is doubt. No, it is insubordination: it is not doubt of religious truth but insubordination against religious authority which is the fault in our misfortune and the cause of it. Disobedience is the secret of the religious confusion of our age."[25] It is interesting that Kierkegaard wrote this at a time when Protestantism, in a decline from strong belief, was adjusting to mid-nineteenth century liberalism, which later gave way to religious socialism. The symptoms that the Danish philosopher mentions are manifestly those displayed in the Catholic church today. He saw it clearly: it is not an honest doubt which is at the source of the decline of obedience, but indifference to a structure that incarnates a faith, and the temptation to defy a derelict authority. Further on in his essay (pp. 103-4), Kierkegaard notes that when the Christian religion ceases to be a "paradox"[26] and a contradiction to the world, then it is "explained back" into the ethical, an easier and easily subjectivized notion. The apostles and Christ himself are then regarded as "geniuses," but no longer as saintly men and God, respectively. A genius is just a "bigger brain," while the saint among men is a paradox to this world. When this "explaining back into the ethical" takes place, Kierkegaard concludes, it is time to say, "good night, Christianity." It is exactly this "ethical," on which Kierkegaard exercises his irony, that corre-

25. Søren Kierkegaard, *On Authority and Revelation: The Book on Adler, or a Cycle of Ethico-Religious Essays* (Princeton: Princeton U. Press, 1955), p. xviii.

26. Paradox for Kierkegaard is a rich concept. It means, first of all, the paradox of Abraham ready to sacrifice Isaac on the command of a God who may be, after all, a cruel player of games. Hence Christianity too is a paradox.

sponds today to "ethical humanism," an expression where the first term sugarcoats the second. One more step, and society's religion becomes "secular humanism."

In the final analysis, the entire enterprise of the church's adjustment to liberal-secular civil society is motivated, first, by the late nineteenth century Modernist movement (with the Americanist movement as its transplanted version in the United States), then by various others regrouped in the "conciliar" church as the nucleus of a "constituent assembly." The idea to "convert" civil society has long been abandoned, something meticulously excluded from the church's tacit contract with modern society. A much more modest ambition animates church leaders, something elaborated from Maritain's proposition of peaceful coexistence with democratic-pluralist society, which is expected merely to guarantee the church a decent old age with an appropriately reduced activity. Cardinal Ratzinger formulates this expectation: There used to be a European-based and legitimate plurality of values; this has now turned into an exaltation of pluralism in which the moral foundation, the sacred, and respect for God are considered irrelevant as community values. The mere request for these values to be reintegrated with public discourse on morality and law is rejected as an offense to "tolerance," in other words a threat from the church. Nevertheless, Ratzinger continues, democracy should understand that its own life is at stake because pluralism is transformed into monism, with totalitarianism at the end of the road. The solution, he concludes, is to return to the Greco-Christian roots of democracy, to refuse the atheistic dogma, and once more to accept God as the ground of the public ethos.[27]

We have said that Ratzinger's thinking, representative of the Vatican's official position, is in the line of Maritain's own systematization of the place of the church in modern democracy. It appears different only because during the half century separating the two men civil society has made enormous strides toward the full implementation of its basic worldview. In Maritain's time the pre-conciliar church was

27. Ratzinger, *Eglise*, pp. 298, 308.

perceived as one which could afford to establish a long-term truce, if not peace, with the world. In Ratzinger's post-conciliar *fin de siècle* the world is in a position to dictate to the church not the terms of the truce, but the conditions of mere acceptability. Why then should triumphant civil society feel threatened by the future? Why should democracy return to its alleged Greco-Christian roots or repudiate atheistic dogma when atheism, in the guise of secular humanism (see Dewey's program), is one of the constituents of its own ideology? If anything, in a short twenty years the optimism of men like Maritain, John Courtney Murray, and Paul VI has been given the lie, and liberal civil society's mentality and practice are approaching those of pagan imperial Rome, as far as the cause of religion is concerned. The compatibility of society and the Christian religion is clearly put in question.

What even straight-thinking Catholic leaders forget—and this lack of realism explains their predicament and unreadiness to react—is that triumphant organizations do not enter into dialogue and compromise. The church did not do so when it was advertised as the *ecclesia triumphans;* neither did the state when it was powerful; civil society too refuses now to walk the road of concessions. Furthermore, Catholic leaders neglect to tackle the ideology against which they struggle with inadequate means. Political society and public policy in modern times are founded on the presupposition that since there is no truth, no participant may claim to possess it. (One should see how university professors run away from making categorical statements!) Political parties, for example, do not represent a "true choice"; their belief focuses on the rotation system through which the alternative party, not claiming truth either, may in turn govern. *Good* or *bad* are not issues; the rule of alternation dictates how modern society functions, contrary to how the church functions. Georges Bernanos, the Catholic novelist, grasped best the church's way when, in the *Diary of the Country Priest,* he has the old country curate, Fr. Torcy, say the following to his young and still inexperienced colleague: "Our poor world is like father Job sitting on the trashheap, covered with wounds. If salt is sprinkled on them it burns, but it also prevents rotting. Observe that we priests are hardly loved, it is not really important that we should be. What is important is that we should be respected, because the first thing the church needs is order. Disorder is always around; the task of you priests, like that of a housewife, is to make order, relentlessly. No illusions: what you accomplish during the day, the devil disperses at night. The night belongs to him."[28] And now a good part of the day too, because—Bernanos seems to say with a physician's diagnosis and a prophet's foresight—the church has for decades abandoned its realism, believing that if it preaches accommodation outside and a loosening of discipline inside, Beelzebub will repent and turn into a dialogue partner.

Option B

Cardinal Ratzinger begins his recent book[29] with a laudatory reference to Romano Guardini's postwar jubilation: "An incalculable event has taken place, the Church is waking up in people's souls!" It seems, if one is to believe Guardini and Ratzinger, that for centuries before 1945, and perhaps since the beginning of Christianity, the church was known by its stern features, its insistence on dogma and legalism, whereas in the past four or five decades, the period culminating in the Vatican Council, the church has rediscovered aspects of charity and humanness, much-needed contact with the world, and the positive side of dialogue and popular participation.

In the same immediate postwar years when Romano Guardini welcomed the reawakening of faith in Christian hearts, what we here call Option B was also adumbrated. What this option consists of may be understood on several levels, some starting out from the church's fear that it was on the point of losing the new postwar world in which Christians and non-Christians live together and where the church must be

---

28. *Journal d'un curé de campagne* (Paris: Club des éditeurs, 1957), p. 10. (My translation.)
29. Ratzinger, *Eglise*, p. 11.

present as a daily spiritual, moral, and cultural influence. While accommodation with civil society (Option A) was increasingly understood as a necessity—a lesson drawn from the recent past, but also from the changing structure of society toward a greater degree of classless egalitarianism—other trends appeared on the horizon that could not be eluded.

The postwar world—in fact, the world since the First World War—had already emerged with a near universal preference for *socialism*, and many Catholic thinkers and intellectuals shared this preference. One of the ingredients of this choice was a sort of ennui with what they saw as a "bourgeois church," judged by them not only to be committed to middle-class values, but also to lack inspiration for renewal in all areas of life, sacramental life included. Socialism promised a new inspiration, opposed to the liberal-capitalist system that appeared excessively materialistic, calculating, and selfish. The working class, suitably romanticized, needed a socialist fraternity where Christian virtues might be cultivated. Whether this was a correct or a false judgment is not here in question. The right approach to the "social problem" seemed to be to detach the "toiling masses" from Marxism in order to guide them to Catholic social principles and, importantly, to strengthen Christianity and the church with the transfusion of fresh proletarian blood. Paul Tillich, one of the Protestant theologians who believed that Christian liberalism à la the nineteenth century was bankrupt, turned with many of his colleagues to the obvious alternative, Christian socialism. Emmanuel Mounier performed a similar operation in Catholic intellectual circles in Europe and South America, along with his group, which had gathered several outstanding personalities (J. Maritain, the Russian ex-Marxist Nikolai Berdyaev, Albert Béguin, and others) around the review *Esprit*.

Guardini's earlier quoted statement turns out to have been rather naive, because what he regarded as the "awakening of faith" was in reality the enthusiasm of the progressive and increasingly openly leftist Christian intelligentsia for what it took to be the unique chance of reconciling the world—seen under the Marxist label—with the Christian faith. Things did not happen as smoothly as pictured here. Clashes multiplied between "bourgeois" and "socialist" Catholicism. The fact that the until then nearly quarantined Soviet Union was among the victors in 1945 decisively contributed to the cause and prestige of Moscow and of the Western proletariat with its communist parties. The stance of progressive Catholic intellectuals, in and out of political parties (among them the multiplying "Christian socialist" parties), may be summed up in this manner: True, a Christian cannot accept Marxism, yet he should not reject out-of-hand the Marxist analysis of the condition of the working class and the remedies it proposes. Actually, such a statement was made by French bishop Mgr. Ancel in 1945, and we find it today repeated and vastly magnified as the core of the message—in books, conferences, and sermons—of South America's "liberation theologians." In fact, the ideology that was a trickle in 1945 has become a torrent four decades later.

In these intervening forty-odd years, the socialist option advocated at the beginning by only a few intellectuals—often as a "third way" between capitalism and Marxism—has become the choice of many; so many, indeed, that they represent today a kind of political party inside the church. To describe its (unofficial) status with some precision one would have to call it an opposition party, not far from becoming the government, and regarded already as a shadow cabinet. The comparison is somewhat forced since the ecclesiastical structure is not, or not yet, democratic and parliamentarian; but the comparison is valid inside many episcopal conferences and in the base communities now in vogue—loosely structured on a reformed model and given to voting on the meaning of Christ's message—that is, on matters pertaining to the competence and sphere of doctrine. More than that, the freedom thus gained is often used by the invisible opposition to widen and strengthen the leftist current. In Catholic pulpits, universities, seminaries, and diocesan bureaucracies quite a few clerics and intellectuals preach the class struggle, armed insurrection, and other forms of leftist violence against society's unjust structure. Many worker-priests, for example, became communists or got married, or both, and hundreds more have been clamoring for "dialogue" with the Marxists as the only way of building a better, and Christian, world.

The church per se has avoided identifying itself with any of these currents, or with the liberal-democratic system and its ideology. However, in view of all the centrifugal trends, what does "the church per se" mean? Certainly not what St. Augustine understood with his *Roma locuta est; causa finita est.* At any rate, it is increasingly hard to locate Rome in Rome—the true will and decision—when almost everything the Vatican decrees is at once contradicted or ignored, and when both contradiction and neglect obtain the backing of local hierarchies and clergy. A well-articulated ecclesiology which identifies the acts of authority and responses to it as set down in canon law is one thing; it is quite another to obey concretely the clauses of canon law. At present, there are ruptures at various points between the Vatican and the local churches, and, what is worse, they are unpredictable from one case to the other, from one bishop and parish to another.

The second observation—concerning the church's avoidance of identification with the new trends—is that the church keeps both irons, or options, in the fire. Neither Option A nor B seems worth a commitment, but both are regarded as means of speaking to the modern world. Yet as the two options are encouraged by the spirit of general adjustment to the prevailing models, so the tension inside the church is bound to grow.

What prompts the partisans of Option B in the direction of socialism? Socialism, let us note, is not necessarily a "leftist" cause, just as liberalism should not be identified with the "Right." Rather, they are twin branches of a this-worldly orientation. According to both, the material world and mankind are accountable to themselves alone, and in proportion to man's domination, supernatural and spiritual considerations are liquidated. In this unilinear, programmed, and desolate philosophy the choice is between *individualism* (only the individual's interests matter, with a minimal public agency to keep order) and *collectivism* (where it is assumed that men pressed together in the mass develop rules of solidarity). It is obvious why the second choice is generally more attractive to Catholic sensitivities than the first. It is true that many liberal Catholics find in individualism a justified economic transposition of the Roman teaching on the salvation of the individual soul, and so on man's freedom to possess goods and dispose of them at will, although within the limits set by public well-being. Yet in the post-1918 collectivist era, reinforced after 1945 by the military successes of the Soviet Union,[30] leftist Catholics had an edge over their adversaries: Is socialism not a secularistic translation of Christian love, charity, and fraternity? Further, liberalism leaves it to chance and the "invisible hand" that a modicum of prosperity emerges in society, though unjustly distributed to the advantage of the rich, the better endowed, and the successful; only socialism is able to establish a link among people and to account for our social nature as taught by Aristotle, the Stoics, and Marx.

Socialism as interpreted by advocates of Option B emphasizes quite obviously a different social structure and, transplanted in religious soil, a greater role of the laity in the church, the "people of God." Prevailing trends in contemporary ecclesiology reinforce this interpretation. The "people of God" (Israel before Christ's resurrection; the church since then) are so named as long as they remain loyal to God and travel the road to Him. In this sense, the name must be deserved: it applies only at certain times, and not when "Israel" falls away from the path of righteousness. Consequently, in this valley of pilgrimage there *is* never a church; it is a church only insofar as it remains with Christ. Leftist theology, including the "liberationist" variety, can thus argue that (a) faithfulness to God is a matter of the right belief and action at a given moment of history, and (b) the message today is delivered through Marxist analysis and the third world, with the quasi-colonial proletariat as the victim (crucified Christ) of capitalism and imperial-

---

30. Fellow travelers after 1945 made statements like this: The fact that Stalin's armies were the first to reach Berlin proves the historical truth of the communist system.

ism. According to this logic, Ernesto Cardenal, a priest and Minister of Culture in the Nicaraguan regime, is correct in explaining that "it is not possible to evade the influence of Marxism, as we cannot commit ourselves to the revolutionary struggle without drawing support from the conclusions of scientific socialism."[31]

All this explains why the leftist or "B" option is not an aberration at the present time, when pluralism, to remain consistent, also must be extended to heterodox viewpoints. This option, with its well thought-out motives and theological arguments, has found a home in ecclesiastical and intellectual circles, where it thrives on the ambiguities of that milieu. On the one hand, spokesmen like Fr. Joseph Tischner, theologian of Cracow, Poland, and friend of the pope, challenge Marxism: "In this country we must live with two realities, Marxism and Christianity; the point at which their dialogue meets is the concept of Work. We must ask Marxism what its ethics of work is. If there is no answer, Marxism has no reason to exist."[32] Fr. Tischner is close to the thinking of John Paul II, and he may even have inspired the encyclical *Laborem Exercens* which stresses *work* as the fundamental value of life in society, the value by which man finds his God-like dignity. In other words, if Marxism is deficient on the ethics of work, the church has one, and teaches it. The church thus answers the great question formulated by the century about the dignity of work, hence about the right of workers to gather in unions independent of the state and its monopolistic-totalitarian ambition. This answer may have been prompted by the situation in Poland, in connection with the rise of Solidarity as a free worker-syndicate. In its entire history the church formulated answers to questions that new varieties of the human problematics demanded: through these questions and answers Rome did not invent new ideas or ideologies; it reached into its doctrinal fund, elaborating the appropriate reply as existing doctrine was applicable to new, concrete situations.

31. "Is Liberation Theology Marxist?" An interview with Ernesto Cardenal in *Crisis* 5 (June 1987): 38.
32. *The Polish Model for the Dialogue* (1980).

On the other hand, however, the texts of liberation theologians emphasize the concrete situation at the expense of doctrine, and they find themselves both facing texts like those of Tischner or the encyclical, and opposing them for their alleged lack of concreteness, immediacy of concern, and political (Marxist) choice. The short quotation from Cardenal is apposite: he visibly goes beyond the Roman intention and accuses it of not acknowledging the history-making truth of Marx's theory. He overlooks the unbridgeable gap between Marxism and the church, calling on the church to adopt the "scientific-socialist" analysis of the workers' condition. From the angle of the leftist vision, the church remains conservative because it allegedly refuses to cut its links with the liberal-capitalist mode of production; as the church sees the issue, liberation theology is blinded by a partial analysis—materialistic and open to violence—and it is unable to formulate an ethics outside the narrow class struggle. Those ecclesiastics and laymen unable or unwilling to weigh these very important nuances are easily swayed by the leftist option; or they at least prepare for their own use a personal solution of the conflict: let the Catholic-Marxists pursue their endeavor; at the end the dialogue will settle matters. Meanwhile, Rome may earn a reputation for tolerance. (We have seen that there have indeed been men who think along these lines, trusting that in the end there will arise a kind of "Marxist Constantine" reconciling Christianity with the political power-wielder.)

Option B is further bolstered with the old argument that Jesus never intended to found a church, so that liberation theologians or other leftists (I quote liberation theologian Jon Sobrino) are free to locate the "church" in any gathering of the poor and exploited, while the Vatican and its Council are "bourgeois institutions." These various quotations indicate that liberation theology is a haphazard intellectual construct whose proponents may not have gone beyond the *Theses on Feuerbach* in their reading of Marx. Whether it is Hans Küng, Hugo Assmann, or Gustavo Gutiérrez, they have formulated an eclectic system reaching into a number of pots to gather material in view of putting together ideologies, modernist fads, popular issues, and self-promoting poses. Their success is to a large extent explicable by the impatience displayed in our age for the latest formulation of a new doctrine by which traditional teaching may be removed from its pedestal.

It would be false, however, to conclude that an impassable wall of separation exists between the church's official conduct and the radical Catholic Left. Rome has always been the home port for many tendencies and schools of thought, although it refused to be identified with any but a handful, such as Thomism or monasticism, theories and practices grown in the native soil. With regard to the matter at hand—liberation theology, encyclicals on labor, the condition of the third-world proletariat, and so on—one should refer to the closest similar situation, the thirteenth century. Historians until recent times were wont to speak of a repressive, feudalized church in that period. The truth is that in the thirteenth century too the church gave several compatible responses to the popular movements which in some cases, and not in others, turned into doctrinal heresies. One of the responses was the Inquisition (not the later Spanish, but the earlier Roman one); the other response was the encouragement given to the newly constituted mendicant orders to concern themselves with the condition of the poor and other potential marginalized categories. In other words, Rome set out to repress the attacks against doctrine, while it undertook to meet society's needs. Observe that the revendicationist heretical movements recruited among the urban population, itself a recent social category at the time. There were among them wealthy burghers (Peter Waldo, St. Francis) and miserably paid textile workers, landless refugee peasants, well-to-do but bored women, and adventurous veterans of foreign wars who could no longer find an occupation. The intellectual and Bible-reading stratum was present then, just as it is in contemporary movements among the rebellious groups in South America or in Poland's Solidarity and its intellectual cover-group, KOR. Its foundation, in fact, had been initiated by Cardinal Wyszinski (1976) calling on independent-minded professors and writers to advise the new labor union. In sum, the church has generally faced social/spiritual movements by distinguishing between the two components, the social need and the spiritual concern. It fought the spiritual and doctrinal deviation, but tried to propose answers to the social discontent.

This policy has become much more problematic today because the "urban-based rebellion" had a different sociocultural base in the thirteenth century from what it has now in the twentieth. Then the "town" was by no means unanimous in its support of the rebellion, and civil society was in its infancy; now civil society is the dominant historical force, the church has no institutional allies, and the city-based media offer shelter—in fact, prominence—to the ecclesiastical dissenters. At any rate, the church is not free in this century to make use of its skills, experience, and wisdom in facing its rebels. It is particularly hindered by the rebels' claim (Option B) to represent the quintessential form of lay apostolate suitable for our time—as the Franciscans and their Left radical wing, the Fraticelli, did in the fourteenth century—that they are closest to the poor, and themselves poor.[33]

While the perspective and the motives had their typical medieval features eight centuries ago, the issue presents itself today under a very similar light. The church insists today, as it did yesterday, on doctrinal integrity about which it cannot make concessions without ceasing to be itself. This is the nonnegotiable part of the day's controversies, whether we call these controversies "October Revolution," the "decline of the church," "accommodation," or "renewal." Basically, the negotiable part is the social issue set in the neo-modern and neo-cultural milieu, and the alliances it entails for the church. The church always needs worldly allies among powerful institutions. We have found that for the longest time this ally was the

---

33. The Dominicans were the "persuaders," combatting heresies with arguments, with the Inquisition, and with the help of the "secular arm" of the state. The popular dictum had it that the Dominicans got their name from "Domini canes latrantes per totum orbem"—God's dogs barking in the whole world—an unflattering description. It belongs to the record that the radical branch of the Franciscans had to be disciplined because it sacrificed doctrine to the social issue, a modern predicament today at all levels of the church.

state, as in the thirteenth century. The two kept order, together shaped a new civilization, and managed the cleansing job that is always necessary where human beings tread (see the passage from Bernanos quoted on pp. 69-70). It is different with the church's partnership (not an alliance!) with civil society. The liberal-pluralist component of society is founded on the double premise that there is no truth, and that this epistemological formula (itself a truth?) guarantees civil peace and prosperity among the metaphysically tamed pressure groups. Thus civil society in its present makeup is impermeable to conversion; in light of rapidly emerging and fading mini-ideologies to which it is open, any permanence or stability is a drawback to be eliminated.

As a consequence, any alliance between the church and civil society, in fact the entire accommodationist policy (Option A), is seen by progressive Catholic intellectuals as a cul-de-sac. As partisans of Option B, they are prompted by the belief that leftist ideas and outlook can be rightfully integrated with the Roman message. It seems to me that this hope of integration is the great "secret" of the controversy. In spite of the comfortable conditions made for the church in liberal society, the impression of the Catholic intelligentsia is that Rome has again sold Jesus for thirty pieces of silver, a deal that is only reversible by ceasing the embarrassing and sinful partnership with capitalism and its materialist pursuits. Is "leftism," or if you wish, "socialism," more attuned to Christianity than liberalism? Since "poor" is a vague term, the Catholic intelligentsia under the wide umbrella of Option B is able to apply it to a variety of categories.

The label has, anyway, little to do with what Jesus meant by it. The poor for him were not the "proletariat" that the earthly kingdom supposedly is able to wrench out of material misery. The poor for Jesus were the abandoned, those whom some debilitating circumstance marginalized. More concretely, in our age they are the pensioners on inflation-bitten, hand-to-mouth income, the lonely, the permanently sick, the silenced and persecuted, those pushed aside and ever-humiliated. Without any doubt, socialism victimizes the same categories of people, and the church, in its leftist option, may not even take cognizance of the real poor, Christ's companions and the objects of his solicitude. Twentieth-century leftist socialism has such a sturdy secular content and such material appetites that Option B may very well turn out to be an illusion on the church's part, no different in its course and consequences from the opposite illusion, the readiness of liberalism to accept holy water. Yet the hope is alive, fed by the daily experience of the power that socialism and the Left in general possess. In 1843 a meeting took place between a few young German leftist Hegelians—Ruge, Marx, and Moses Hess—and some older French socialists, the excommunicated abbé Lamennais, Étienne Cabet, and Louis Blanc. The first group, frustrated revolutionaries, had crossed the Rhine to Paris in the hope of finding senior interlocutors in the city where some half century before the Great Revolution had smashed the old structure and the old god. To their painful astonishment, Marx and his friends found themselves before a wall of refusal: Lamennais and his colleagues could not envisage a socialism without religion and rejected Marx's heaven-storming atheistic enterprise.

The answer then must be "no" to the question of whether socialism (leftism) is better attuned to Christianity than is liberalism. This answer is irrelevant, however, because in the minds of present-day Catholic leftists, as in the mind of their ancestor Lamennais, religion and socialism remain linked. These Catholic leftists, ecclesiastic and lay, are committed to combining the cause of the variously exploited with the gospel message. In fact, as enthusiasm for the Marxist solution is waning worldwide, they may be the rearguard Marxists, and as such may be as fanaticized and intolerant as the Marxist vanguard was decades ago. They find a reassurance in what E. Cardenal said in the earlier quoted interview: "Atheism is not the cause of the conflict between Christianity and Marxism, but is rather the link between them. What Marxism calls atheism is basically the negation of an idol, which sometimes bears the name of God. I think that the proclamation of the Gospel is sometimes nearer to an atheistic point of view than to traditional religious attitudes, for when God calls us to judgment, as Jesus Christ told us, it will not be faith in God or lack of it which will decide, but whether we loved our neighbor or hated him during our lifetime."[34] This statement could be the summary of the Marxist-Christian dialogue, with the advantage clearly going to the Marxists: they claim a religious stature for Marxism and give the Christians a bad conscience for their alleged idolatry.

It so happens that I met a typical representative of Option B, Brazilian bishop Helder Camara—at one time a much-displayed specimen of the international Catholic-Marxist Left—lecturing with a wooden pectoral cross (he did not miss calling my attention to it) when this was a symbol of commitment to the poor, and a red carnation in his cassock. Our four-hour conversation took place at his residence, Olinda, near the sullen and violence-filled port city of Recife, in Brazil's northeast. The bishop lashed out against churches behind what had become the Iron Curtain, "feudal power-structures, allies of aristocrats and landowners," he said. "They deserved the Soviet occupation and the material destitution; this will teach them Christian virtues." Dom Helder was willing to engage the revolution in order to relieve the misery of Brazil's notoriously poor provinces, even if that meant a communist takeover. This was in 1966; the term "liberation theology" was not yet widely known. The inspiration, however, was powerfully feeding the Christian-leftist program.

Mgr. Helder Camara is one example, but he typifies the contemporary situation in which the post-conciliar church finds itself. The Council of Vatican II has been hailed as the opening of a new era. The "opening of the Vatican's windows" had been planned as a way of facilitating contact with the outside world. Yet acts of this magnitude follow their own logic, not necessarily any initial intention, and their course can hardly be controlled. One illustration of this logic is that today, twenty-five years after my conversation with Dom Helder, many bishops all over the world, including the United States,

---

34. "Is Liberation Theology Marxist?" p. 38.

speak *his* language and often go well beyond his then revolutionary stand. This is because whatever the vision of the assembled church fathers had been, the Council's decisions, decrees, and their consequences were perceived by the rest of the world as a license for partnership with the powerful of tomorrow (already today!), in a world shifting politically and culturally toward the Left. In the context of the Council at the time of its sessions, the early 1960s, the two candidates for the partnership were *liberal democracy*, seemingly triumphant but based mostly on its prosperity and not on any heartwarming ideal, and *leftist socialism*, credited with bearing in its womb humanism and fraternity.

Thus leftist socialism, diffuse but stronger than it was at the time when the Council convened, is not one narrowly defined political program; it is rather a wide spectrum of subcultures, intellectual cliques, and political ideologues. A friendly handshake with one, an intention of rapprochement, brings the church into contact with a multitude of micro-worlds, parts of a loose network sharing the same worldview. Concretely, the Vatican's *Ostpolitik* (we are not discussing here whether it is positive or negative in its effects), which in earlier times would have been an enterprise limited to diplomatic moves—as was papal policy vis-à-vis the sultans in the fifteenth century—involves an indefinitely self-enlarging series of contacts with leftist organizations. These organizations, cultural sects, academic pressure groups, international juries of books, films, and festivals live in a symbiotic relationship with the propagandists of Marxist regimes, and are not adverse to the ideals they profess. No clear line can be drawn in this age of instant communications: the unsaid word gets interpreted, acquiring weight and direction in the process. A crude example: a sympathetic message to homosexuals is interpreted as part of a certain language, at the other end of which is a dialogue outlined with terrorist organizations.

Option B is perceived according to this analysis as being less a consciously programmed, single-minded, and purposefully elaborated policy, and more a network of partly planned initiatives plus their multiform and unforeseen by-products. It is debatable whether this "soft option" is due to a conscious decision or to the general inertia that has taken hold of the church at its center and spread to the periphery. The weakening of the fabric of religious faith and the transfer of loyalties (clerical and episcopal loyalties included) to ideologies and mundane systems mainly benefits the current which is irresistibly driving the Catholic intelligentsia towards the amorphous upper bourgeoisie whose lifestyle they largely admire and would like to share. It is only an apparent paradox that the same people condemn bourgeois consumerism, aspiration for opulence, and hedonism. In reality, the progressive wing of the church yields to the dominant current of the bourgeoisie with the same gusto as did their predecessors, the perfumed and bewigged abbés and bishops in the salons of eighteenth-century France, where the talk was about atheist tracts and the coming revolution. Above all, Option B must remain a seamless garment: if the alliance with new leftism is given up at any one point, the rest of the fabric becomes undone. Facing the new powers—media, public opinion, human rights advocates, liberal society and its socialist intelligentsia—the church becomes a quasi-prisoner of its own experiment in partnership. Or, as the semi-repentant Jacques Maritain wrote in his life summary, *The Peasant of the Garonne:* through the open windows the church got a severe influenza.

The Seduction of the Church

On the level of the church's supernatural interests the alliances and partnerships described as Option A and Option B must be weighed as methods of protecting and safeguarding doctrine, while negotiating in historical terms the social, cultural, and other adjustments to prevailing circumstances. Nobody in particular made the decision that this should be done, that a subtle balancing of possibilities should separate the heart of the matter from the parts of the accommodation. There is no bank vault to protect the valuables; there is no outer envelope and a secret treasure inside. There is, however, the raison d'être of the church: Christ's message and promise; and there are the believers, perplexed by the counter-doctrine preached from pulpits. As the believers receive the secularist and accommo-dationist stone in the place of the life-giving bread, some remain in their pews by tradition, routine, or hope. Others leave quietly or slam the door. In sum, the church may gradu-ally become irrelevant.

Rome is now perceived, like other declining but still world-spanning institutions (empires and religions) of the past, as a huge body acting in a twilight zone. This does not mean that the issues of survival or decline are not discernible, only that they are allowed their veil and mask. Otherwise strong action would be urgent. At times the needed words for moral guidance are indeed spoken, but at other times fatal weak-nesses in words and action are obvious. Examples of the first: in 1968 Paul VI, perhaps the weakest pope in history (his predecessor called him "Hamlet" for his hesitations and post-ponements), astounded the world and many churchmen[35] with his encyclical *Humanae Vitae*, a gauntlet of defiance thrown in the face of a society drowned in moral filth. It happened again with the same pope's *Credo*, a crystal-clear statement of Catholic truth, and again when John Paul announced his devo-tion to the Virgin upon his accession to the pontificate. And in February 1987 came the publication of the *Instruction* against biogenetic manipulation of parenthood and the birth of chil-dren. These Roman acts were scandals, moral shocks to an immoral society and a derelict clergy.

To give examples of the tolerance, even encouragement, of this dereliction is much more difficult because they have been an avalanche in the past twenty-five years. Many of them have already been mentioned in these pages. Going beyond them, however, let us focus on an issue where inertia suggests a profound lack of spiritual and cultural inspiration. We dis-cussed briefly the church's thirteenth-century strategy of safe-guarding doctrine while meeting a new society's deepest yearnings for a place under the sun. While the Roman Inquisi-tion was dealing, in the times' often brutal methods, with

---

35. Cardinal Bernardin called it in private "that goddamn encyclical."

far-reaching doctrinal deviations and heresies, Rome also sent the mendicant orders out into the world, speaking the language of the little people, getting near them in their daily lives. Monastic life as such was not thereby revolutionized (Benedictines, Cistercians, and others kept their earlier formulated rules), but new approaches and objectives were added to it according to the new needs and style.

This seems impossible today. A similarly vast project could entail the partial turning around of liberation theology toward an order directed to the issues of the day, some modern form of the thirteenth-century Franciscans that preserves orthodoxy and repudiates the Marxist underbrush. This could be undertaken through dialogue, to be sure, but it must be a dialogue firmly conducted from the point of view of the faith *and* institutional continuity. Let us repeat Kierkegaard's diagnosis: it is authority that is lacking; hence the insubordination.

In the same spirit the church could approach the proliferating sub-ideologies: feminism, anarchism, low culture, drug addiction, and the like. There are no sure formulas and paths to positive results, but a clearly declared spiritualization of civil society's degenerating culture would offer more than an alternative—it would be a powerful center of attraction in the face of the present misery of vagrant culture. Let us restate the obvious: the church itself is the first to suffer from a social dereliction principally manifested in the underestimation of the church's own supernatural resources. Should the church activate these resources, break the "social contract" which reduces it to spiritual impotence, and step in front of the world with its demands, things would begin clearing up. After all, Rome knows that the situation it faces is but the latest surge of religious heresies disguised as political and cultural challenges. The old reactions to them would prove valid again.

Option B appears to many as the lesser of two evils. We must assume that at one or several times some highly placed personalities have surveyed the postwar decades and concluded that Western democracies are on a historic retreat and that socialism is advancing, both in the Western world and elsewhere. That analysis is not only the Vatican's; it has been made by many. In my estimation,[36] socialism has become an ideological amalgam with such ingredients as Marxism, populism, military ambitions, national survival, semicontrolled economy, anti-Western sentiments, and mistrust of communist regimes, plus of course a variety of local demands. Gamal Nasser of Egypt was such a "socialist," in addition to other more recent leaders in such numbers that they by now form a type—ideologically "faceless socialists," as I called them—products of certain circumstances like decolonization and mass poverty. "Faceless socialism" can be said to be a tamed version of hard or Marxist communism; as the latter was spreading and awakening expectations, it also had to adjust to situations which contradicted its central dogmas. The way events unfolded it was as if the church had been waiting to meet the diluted form of Marxism in the manner in which it had met the diluted form of imperial Rome—let us call it "Constantinism"—in order to dialogue with it. Statements and policies issued by an increasing number of church officials favor this kind of socialism as a sign of the future. In the process, these utterances, documents, and gestures have the effect of assimilating the church to a generally leftist attitude, as it used to be assimilated, in reality and in people's minds, to a generally rightist attitude. The true significance of the Council is neither doctrinal nor pastoral: it is the liquidation of one form of political option and the adoption of another one.

Thus Option B is not in itself a dialogue with the Kremlin's masters, not a generalized *Ostpolitik*, nor the statements on liberation theology—it is all of these plus the move into a new cultural environment. This explains why the Council, in the three years of its duration, did not mention the gulag, why the American bishops have not listened to the internal opponents in Nicaragua, why the French bishops multiply their support of a "multi-cultured," Moslem-settled France, why

36. See my book *Le socialisme sans visage* (Presses Universitaires de France, 1976).

Catholic universities tolerate homosexual organizations and pornographic publications on their campuses.[37]

Rome occasionally criticizes these acts, words, and measures. The fact, however, is that the Vatican keeps a generally hands-off attitude, as if suspending judgment. The question in people's minds is this: Does the church not contradict and condemn these one-directional novelties because it lacks the moral and cultural courage to swim against the current, or because it prefers that a cloud of equivocation should cover its own itinerary? It is hard to know. Meanwhile, the believers' confusion spreads, since Rome says one thing, the local bishops another, priests and teachers a third. Where is the church's *universality* in all of this? Can an institution speak in many tongues and make utterances as if they were coming from conflicting forces? I have met—we all have—too many perplexed "little people" to think that this is a tolerable situation, unless we are contemporaries of a church "in transition": between pre- and post-Council, authority and democracy, one partnership and another. When the church converted pagans, half of its success was due to its uncompromising attitude which pointed to a rocklike faith. The work of God was accomplished by Hebrew prophets and Christian missionaries, not through ecumenical dialogue with local idols but through trust in the Lord. The world, the idols, and the hearts of men have not changed.

---

37. Georgetown University's attitude is a case in point. The homosexual organization on campus has been tolerated for years, and has been given campus facilities for its activities. When it demanded more funds and took the case to court, the Jesuit university began protesting, then yielded, because the financing of its building program was threatened. Imagine a pre-conciliar Catholic university with homosexual dances! This is not "cultural accommodation"; it is connivance with sin. At Fordham University, also a Jesuit institution, the authorities have been unwilling to take measures against a professor who was writing for a pornographic magazine. One excuse for not taking measures was that the law does not specify what is meant by pornography or obscenity.

CHAPTER FOUR

Dark Clouds or Silver Lining?

The object of Option B is a new partnership initiated, according to our analysis, by the church, with the intention of protecting the sacred deposit of doctrine through a worldly arrangement. In this view, the Second Vatican Council did not simply and erratically drift into the post-conciliar radical excesses, but was the product of a more or less willed and planned switch from the bonds of the "social contract" signed with liberal civil society to an attempt at a new partnership with socialism and the Left. This is a very controversial diagnosis of Vatican II, likely to be sharply criticized by all three entities mentioned: liberal society, the church, and socialists; it merely demands to be regarded at this point as a hypothesis capable of explaining the recent and present course of events.

The triangular phenomenon involves a historic move on the church's part, a vast change of alliances. In the nineteenth century the church exchanged, as partner, throne for republic; then, in the last hundred years or so, it moved from the conservative and liberal bourgeoisie to the radical Left and to mass democracy. The situation further involved the church's decision how to shape and partly control the new partnership, in view of implementing long-range policy in the temporal order. Such moves on the part of the church only occur when its adversary has become "tamed" through time and erosion so that Rome may enter into dialogue with it. We are then witnessing the taming of the Left (for example, away from the very

aggressive forms of Marxism), which facilitates the many contacts between its various forms and the church. The whole
operation, of course, must be conducted by a clear wisdom,
weighing the safety of guardianship over faith and doctrine.
Yet it cannot be taken for granted at the present time and at this
stage in history that the church possesses the informed will
and unity of purpose implied in Option B. The masterful
history-making moves effected by the church in the past offer
no guarantee that Rome has not now become a second-rate
actor on the world scene, unable to conceive, let alone execute,
a sustained policy. Thus, realistic as it may seem, Option B is
by no means assured of success; it is threatened, among other
things, by illusions, by an excess of zeal, and by an initial
position of weakness.

Taking the course of Option B has different but no less
weighty consequences than its opposite, but it is not an option
like the church's earlier ones. Until now, partnership with
historical institutions (like the state) or with live forces (feudal-
ism, bourgeoisie, pagan kingdoms, social classes, or alien cultures such as the Chinese culture in the seventeenth century)
followed from the unraveling of new power relations in which
the church, permitted to move near the center, was welcomed
as a valuable auxiliary and ally. The only permanent alliance
has been with the state, due to the common responsibilities of
the two institutions sharing power—a power based on the
commonly held concept of authority and the common need for
society's moral foundations and vitality. As Fustel de Coulanges wrote, the *res publica* promoted universal values but so
did the church. The two spheres of power, however, were
clearly differentiated at their core, into spiritual and temporal.
To govern a community of men, both respond to the necessity
of organizing the community through laws, customs, social
networks, and institutional articulation, and both provide it
with moral requirements: right conduct, contribution to the
common good, and openness to transcendence.[1]

---

1. Nevertheless, there is no exact symmetry between the functions of
the two powers. St. Thomas teaches that the state has no right to the whole

Now with the dissociation and dislocation of the two spheres of authority—church and state—and the consequent weakening of both (the objective and essential achievement of liberalism), the church no longer finds a stable ally among the clashing groups of civil society. Or at least it has no partner with similarly overarching interests. In other words, when the church "opted" for the contractual partnership with civil society—a contract vehemently resisted by Pius IX and a number of prominent Catholic thinkers—it did not simply shift the alliance from one institution to another, from state to society. It remained without an ally, without another overarching institution which, for being of the temporal order, possessed a public and moral dimension with universal values, as Fustel de Coulanges said. Civil society is not a historical and organic successor of the state, but its opposite. Its interest is not focused on the moral consolidation of the community; instead it expects some kind of morality to emerge as the haphazard result of its individual members' material success. Therefore it exalts the aggressive individual and hopes that public morality, or rather a public orderliness of procedures, will be the by-product of the material (economic) contentment of the largest possible number (Jeremy Bentham). Correspondingly, it downplays the significance of such networks of society that develop according to tradition, loyalty, and a love of permanence.

All this means that partnership with civil society, and therefore Option A, is not rooted in any commonly held concept of the community and its communal and moral foundation. The church today seems sociologically "floating" in a void because the social contract regulating its operations truncates the plenitude of its functions and renders questionable its mission. This partnership has rather the character of an "arrangement," a legal and legalistic deal in which the church is confronted by civil society and its unstable, evanescent ideology.

Given these circumstances, can Option B be regarded as genuine, as an alternative to the earlier option? It may be that

---

man, only to the part by which he is a citizen. In the matter of other activities man is free, master of himself, his time, his associations, and his interests.

the church's present predilection for the Left is not so much dictated by strategy—the search for a new, powerful ally—as by the ideological radicalization of liberal society. One may wonder whether the new ally—the Left, varieties of socialism, the new "culture" and lifestyle, plus the various issues which keep leftist indignation in the state of protest—actually needs the church as an ally when (*a*) the church has undergone a kind of laundering at the hands of liberal society, and (*b*) the Left itself has no thought of organizing a true community with the common good *(bonum commune, res publica)* at its center.

From the church's point of view today's situation is heir to the last 100 to 150 years, insofar as most of the church's earlier prerogatives have been taken over, at times confiscated, by liberal society and its agencies: in education, moral guidance, cultural ideals, civic discipline, the entire tonus of society. At times this was done through legal means, and at other times by pressure, but generally through the mere fact that the dominant position fell to civil society. But let us emphasize that this was not done by some long-term conspiracy of occult interests, illuminists, freemasons, and militant utopians, as many people on the Right claim. These elements certainly played a leading role in the secularization of society, in the privatization of the church, and in the expropriation of the state.[2] For lack of a better term, we may call the combination of all the factors which effected the change "forces of history," God's will, the mysterious power which regulates events. It remains that the separation, and separate weakening, of state and church has left the church politically in an unanchored position, between Option A, which daily reduces its mission to that of a social agency and excludes it from moral and other

---

2. The Estates General called together on the threshold of the French Revolution had, in the Third Estate, 469 freemasons out of a total of 578 members, and in the First Estate (nobility), 90 freemasons out of 300 members. The Second Estate (episcopate and clergy) had by definition no freemasons in its ranks, at least not openly, but it had such radical members as Abbé Sieyès, the motor of the Revolution in its initial stages, and Bishop Talleyrand.

decision making, and Option B, the representatives of which may prove indifferent to the church's extended hand.

The Church as Interest Group

Thus the question is this: Why should the coming world—if it will be organized by the Left, as the partisans of Option B expect and welcome—want to have the church as an ally, which means a sharer of power? As far as liberal society is concerned, we saw that it extends a helpful hand only to dissenters of the church, particularly when they appear at the dialogue table dressed in the full regalia of their office, for then they seem to commit the entire church to their own dissenting position. On the face of it, there is no reason why this attitude could not be adopted also by societies permeated by socialist ideology. But there is also another point. In the game of politics an ally is useful only to the extent that it brings numerous and disciplined troops to the alliance. This was the case in the cooperation between state and church: the state could fully trust the clergy under ecclesiastical authority, and the clergy knew it could count on the "secular arm." Now that the church has gone through the flattening process demanded by Option A as part of the social contract between liberal ideology and Roman interests, it is no longer able to provide a disciplined clergy. At one time it was taken for granted (it was indeed the "great secret" of the future) that the new industrial society with its uprooting of peasants and their traditional way of life would need a new public belief replacing Christianity. Men like Kant, Claude Henri Saint-Simon, Auguste Comte, and Emile Durkheim expected an undogmatic and un-doctrinal—let us say a rational, even scientific—Christianity to bring to society the new principle of cohesion. Comte went so far as to write in the 1850s to the General of the Jesuits, a body he admired for its integral faith, loyalty to the pope, and single-purpose action, offering him partnership in the task of implementing the political-organizational aspects of his own positivistic philosophy. He received no reply from him or from Tsar Nicholas, whose state-run church (through the procurator of the Synod) he also admired.

Obviously, nobody would think of making such an offer to Rome today, when all realize that within one hundred years the church has lost its authority and cohesion, except for disciplinary measures exercised against the politically impotent rightist remnant which is chained to the church by its unconditional loyalty and thus ready to take punishment with a quasi-masochistic passiveness. It is, however, instructive to remember that not long ago the very thinkers of modernism regarded church discipline as a model more reliable than military discipline itself because it is inspired by an otherworldly faith. However, their successors, radicals of this age, take good note of the fact that even church cohesion can relax, discipline be thrown to the wind, and disobedience spread like an epidemic. If any lesson is drawn from this unexpected situation, it is learned by liberals as well as by socialists: for whatever reasons—reasons differently interpreted—the church has begun its process of self-dissolution. Its politization[3] (descent into the mundane sphere, not as a guide but as an ideological participant, almost as a political party on the Left) makes it in the long run useless as an ally. To be sure, the church is still a power in public life, and to this extent its various social services are not spurned; but the nature of the services is circumscribed by the other partner and by growing public indifference.

Is this the case only with liberal society? More brutally than liberal society, a socialist party bureaucracy in its exclusive decision-making capacity would know how to set limits to the sphere within which the church may participate. If, as we have repeatedly said, the relationship between church and liberal civil society is governed by a debilitating social contract, the relationship between church and socialist bureaucracy may be described as one between the keeper of historical truth and an erratic wanderer in darkness. The relationship between Marxism and the church was well characterized by Fr. Jozef Tischner of Krakow, adviser to John Paul II: "The communist

---

3. "Mundanization" or "this worldization" (*Diesseitigkeit*) would be more precise terms.

conviction is that all that exists at the present moment is merely
a preparation for a better future. In relation to this, all that is
here and now, is not yet real. Truth is in the process of being
born. To sum it up, that which does not exist is more real than
that which does."[4] Since history, the highest instance, guarantees the communist future, it is more real than the Christian
present that history has rejected.

The reason why Option B appears in a seductive light is
that where the Left is not in power ("is not yet"), its adepts use
the tag of culture to describe it, a camouflaged way of describ-
ing the socialist dream. Comparatively, then, liberal society
appears as the opposite of culture—that is, exclusively materialistic and tied to capitalism. The socialist regime of the
"future" basks in its commitment to culture and the aesthetic
quality of life. Thus whatever the Left proposes has at once an
aura of lightness, generosity, and creative endeavor—over
against the rigidity and crassness of all earlier forms, including
the Western liberal society. This is the substance of the Italian
Marxist Antonio Gramsci's theory, elaborated in the 1920s and
1930s. He understood that the self-glorifying bourgeoisie,
having secured for itself the material means of production,
would fall easy prey to the blandishments of leftist "culture"
and its radical representatives. This apparent focus on culture
by the Left has contributed, more than other factors, to the
socialists' popularity in the eyes of the opinion-making intelligentsia. Yet when socialist regimes are actually installed in
power, culture is the first to suffer from party policy and
ideological uniformization. This recurrent fact, however, is not

4. Interview with Thadeusz Witkowski in *Studium Papers* (1988), re-
printed in *Crisis* (June 1988). In my book *La Gauche vue d'en face* (Paris: Seuil,
1970), I analyzed the Left generally in much the same way: permanent
restlessness and agitation to bring to reality a utopian image; when realized, it
is at once regarded as ossified and rigid, while the dialectical movement of
history prepares the next utopia; and so on and on. As a consequence, the Left
benefits by the presentation of impossible objectives, thus placing the Right in
an unfavorable light for its alleged immobility, that is, for its insistence on the
concrete and the here-and-now. For this reason, the collapse of communist
regimes cannot be considered as the end of Marxist and generally leftist
inspiration to action.

understood by the intelligentsia and its bourgeois enthusiasts in their endless debate to find out just what happened, what went wrong with the central inspiration of a leftist society.

Underneath the comfortable umbrella of high-sounding slogans, leftist regimes sharpen the politization of all issues between those who are with them and those who are against. Every situation is defined as conflictual, the other side being ipso facto condemned by history and ready to be dismantled or destroyed. The Left takes no responsibility for executing history's judgment, since verdict and execution are inscribed in the laws of dialectics. Struggle, especially class struggle (the sharpest of all), is the matrix out of which the new, real world is bound to arise, and leftist regimes are the Socratic midwives helping the process along to its destiny. All others (the bourgeoisie, the church, the family) are merely hindering the process, perhaps unknowingly, though that does not mitigate their guilt.

From all this it follows that at its core the radical Left can never accept from the church anything but a tactical and unequal alliance. The "truth" of the Left is to be realized in the ever postponed future, a truth always out of reach. Those who oppose the Left are therefore labelled history's waste, "stupid" in the sense that their class interest veils from their eyes the true source of their opposition. They cannot even be enlightened, let alone pardoned for their class-influenced false consciousness. They are sentenced to the "trashheap of history," and the leftist party bureaucracy merely executes the sentence. The contrast with the Christian worldview is striking. Consider that for the Christian not even Lucifer is an incarnation of evil. He is a fallen angel, and neither his "change of heart" nor the ultimate salvation of those damned in hell is ruled out. For Christians, evil is not a reality, but a choice that freedom makes possible; it is, so to speak, the shadow of creation's greatest gift: being. For Christianity, as also for Plato, the "turning around" is always expected; evil, even original sin, does not destroy the divine face in man's soul.

Rome operates under the possibly mistaken belief that its

signals are favorably interpreted by those to whom they are addressed: the Left, and in general the emerging new world. Proponents of Option B should not assume that the political authorities of the post-liberal era will necessarily grasp the church's proferred hand. The central assumption is that the Left-ward orientation of the new era will help the church survive in the next few centuries. As a partner, the church does not now possess trump cards—it is unable to deliver either a vigorous, unifying public philosophy or troops to propagate and protect it. The times when the church was able to do both are gone. The first such time was when the church secured a relatively smooth transition from Roman imperial power to the new world of the barbarians; the second time, in the twelfth and thirteenth centuries, was when the Dominicans and Franciscans renewed the faith and its forms in the post-feudal civilization; the third was when the Counter Reformation was entrusted to the Jesuits. There are no such forces of renewal perceptible in today's religious landscape.

There are also other points to consider. "Post-liberal" and "post-Western" mean, if words have a sense, *socialist* and *third world*. The initiators and executants of Option B were encouraged in their quest and their new perspective by what they had learned from the first centuries of Christianity, when the new religion had the vigor of conquering the empire; and again when the church entered a two-centuries long agony, disengaging from the ruins and taking over the religious, civic, and cultural education of the new nations. This was such a civilizational bravura that the church has ever since been confident of its ability to perform it again. A new opportunity has arisen. The Western-liberal world is unquestionably on the decline, so the church looks to the third world and to the regimes which wear all sorts of identifying tags (or none at all), but among which "socialism" has become the common denominator.

And it is true that, on the surface, the church's physical and political relocation away from the West may seem promising. Yet the "relocation" has serious limits, and not just geographical ones. We have argued that "socialist" regimes generally reject the Christian religion on a philosophical ground. Third-world regimes are more receptive to the Protestant churches which appear as a local initiative, not coordinated from a politically weighty Western center. Furthermore, the vast areas of the third world are still, and will remain for a long time, permeated by the spirit—in fact, by huge blocks— of religions like Islam, Hinduism, Confucianism, Buddhism, and animism, all of which elicit powerful loyalties. Roman penetration in those areas (not the public relations kind of the Assisi gathering) appeared promising as long as the church came or seemed to come not only with the cross of Christ, but also with the prestige of the Roman empire, later of the "Roumis" (Romans, that is, Westerners), and more recently of the imperial nations like England and France. Rome could boast for 1500 years of building churches in all parts of the world, and around them little enclaves and institutions like schools, universities, hospitals, workshops, orphanages, and shelters for the old, for unwed mothers, and for the sick. In other words, it was a social, and so a political presence which, moreover, required the local converts to burn the old gods and worship the new—that is, drop their traditions and adopt alien ways. Most of this, incidentally, was positive, as when polygamy was abolished in Africa, or when the practice of burning widows on the dead husband's funeral pyre in India was forsaken.

Many of these new ways, by now routine, will undoubtedly continue, but the signs of change and opposition are multiplying on the part of Buddhist bonzes, Hindu priests and gurus, Moslem ulemas—and the governments behind them. We have said that these governments are *not* states in the Western sense, which means, first of all, that they do not acknowledge as valid the dual nature of power, temporal and spiritual. They arrogate both spheres to themselves. It is of course not necessary to instruct Catholic missionaries in the philosophical monism of most African and Asian populations. They have been well aware, in their work and proselytizing among them, that most non-Western people do not cut existence up into segments or separate the realms of mind, body, and spirit.[5] Hence, no concept of the duality of power exists in their political universe except for a thin, surface veneer on tribes, sultanates, and charismatic regimes left there by Western impact that will fade with time. What remains more solidly is a still generally hospitable reception to spirituality as such, though it is not often translated into concretely institutional aspects, let alone into works of charity as understood and practiced in the Christian West. The church has, therefore, a positive although limited place given it in sufferance by the third-world countries. Perhaps the place of the church in the third world prefigures its future in general. Such a place can only be held on condition that the church renounces any political ambition and remains an auxiliary institution in the slow transformation of third-world societies according to as yet unforeseeable patterns. Any other aspiration would inspire jealousy on the part of local religious authorities and the governments themselves. A good illustration of this is Egypt, where the Coptic (Christian) population is surrounded by distrusting Moslems, such a distrust that a Copt can occupy a high position in government—e.g., the present minister of foreign affairs, Boutros Galli—only if the post is nominally held by a Moslem. This, in spite of the fact that the Copts are from the pharaohs' time Egypt's original population.

It is important that we sum up the future state of things, outside liberal societies and outside the West, as it appears from the church's point of view. Unable to count on political allies, the church will be obliged to withdraw from the political scene and limit itself to the status of a public organization, whether according to the residual liberal agenda or under socialist regimes. The partisans of Option B do not necessarily see it this way. They may share our diagnosis as far as liberal society is concerned, but they are optimistic with regard to the

5. In addition to personal observations of local beliefs and mental structure, I found a number of enlightening works about the subject (Catholic presence in the third world) by Ismail Quiles, Maurice Heinrichs, H. van Straelen, etc.

church's fate in socialist society. Why so? Because they observe and deplore the liquidation of the state in liberal society,[6] but trust that socialism is bound to reconstruct the state just as it constructed a strong central authority in communist countries. In fact, these clerical and episcopal observers see in Marxism a circuitous way of reasserting a strong, unifying public philosophy which is so sorely lacking in the liberal West. They seem to say: Rather an evil general belief which can be combated and eventually "turned around" (again, the conversion of pagan Rome!) than no public belief at all, as with liberalism and its philosophical core that rejects man's transcendental ends.

However, this is forgetting that what the Marxists and other leftists constructed is not the state but a party, a kind of indoctrinating and conditioning machine which does not share power. The basic principles of socialism have not changed, although matters in several countries have turned out contrary to principles after decades of oppression. In Poland and other Soviet satellites, as well as in the Soviet Union's Asian republics, the Catholic church and Islam have been making real strides forward. Likewise, in third-world countries socialist regimes accept the church's presence and auxiliary services on a temporary and limited basis. What happens is that social and civic discipline is supplied by the local religious institutions and by practices based on an immemorial tradition. In fact, many third-world nationalists reason that the influence of liberalism turns their societies into wild anarchies, poor copies of the West. But socialism, if adopted, would be adjustable to the old traditions of clan,

---

6. Archbishop Rembert Weakland gave voice recently to these regrets. Before an audience, Weakland said that Americans are "hyper-individualists," reject talk about economic justice, and find the concept of the common good meaningless. He added that Americans are scared of collectivism, and that the wealthy among them "get nervous" about social justice. The archbishop wants the episcopate "to discern those voices in society which somehow are the voices of God's people" (*Crisis*, June 1988). Weakland's language is rudimentary, even primitive, but an unconscious Option B comes through it rather clearly. If faced with collectivism, he would undoubtedly reject it, yet he might be one of those clerics willing to go along with the socialist project.

tribe, and local methods of production, and would not break up the traditional ties of village solidarity. These nationalists therefore become socialist not through any commitment to Marxism, but from the reasoning that this combination of nationalism and socialism is the best preserver of a people's identity against the pervasive influence that Western liberal ideology exerts.

In sum, what in the West has been a slow, gradual process of privatizing the church (separation from the state, the "social contract," the clear favor shown to secular humanism in replacing Christianity in the public square) becomes a rapid and brutal process in the socialist world. The consequence is practically the same: the church's exclusion from the political realm. Cardinal Ratzinger is of course correct when he states that "Catholic social doctrine is meant to promote optimal models of development, suited to given human realities in a historical situation."[7] It remains to be seen, however, whether such models are consonant with the will of governments and the public opinion they express or manipulate. For the Catholic model necessarily includes transcendence, which may invalidate its acceptability in regimes having their own religion or ideology.

Yet the church is upon the threshold of a new field of action. It expects a renewal of faith in socialist regimes and parts of the third world, having given up the liberal, tired, and cynical West. It is a substantial occurrence, surrounded by many signs. Here are a few as indicators.

1. Large areas of Africa, Oceania, and even "Catholic" South America have become territories of conversion to Protestantism, often to its fundamentalist sects. This is true of Angola, Brazil, and East Asia, but also of the Chilean middle class, sophisticated enough to be disheartened by the church's own post-conciliar reforms that invariably lead to turmoil, apostasy, and political radicalism;

2. The conversion of many Western intellectuals and

7. Ratzinger, *Eglise, oecumenisme et politique* (Paris: Fayard, 1987), p. 356.

youth to Islam, which offers a more simple theology, but also a greater fervor, discipline, and political vigor;[8]

3. While a certain number of Anglicans, including clergy, turn to Rome, scandalized by uncontrolled "reformism" like women's ordination, some deeply worshipful Catholics begin attending Greek Orthodox services, attracted by the Eastern churches' capacity for silent suffering and witnessing, and their traditional integrative liturgy and sacred, not "modernized" (as in the case of Roman liturgy), language and music;

4. Masses of Christians fall away from the church and become adepts of Eastern religions and illuminist creeds, justifying the Western advance of Buddhism and its variants.[9] In an increasing number of cases they insist on "dis-registering" from parishes and diocesan offices in order to lend a stronger emphasis to their cessation of faith;

5. Less controversially, the church owes it to itself to be increasingly present among non-Western Catholics—for example, Ukrainians, the church in India, and the Maronites in Lebanon. The latter especially receive the first shocks of renascent Moslem assaults in Arab territories. In the new circumstances (of Western retreat), the church is expected to involve itself in the affairs of distant Catholic territories and enclaves and become a local participant, unlike in the past when a more imperial Vatican could settle matters through distant diplomacy.

These are some of the examples which militate in favor of the church's more intensive presence in, and preoccupation with, areas designated as third world. This may also stem the alienation and actual departure of silent majorities as well as elites in directions indicated above: Protestantism, Islam, East-

8. As a not so isolated example, I mention the case of A. S., a Brooklyn Jew, ex-leftist, visitor to Castro's Cuba, and participant in all ungodly actions (his words), who slowly changed his life orientation when he (a) understood the futility of Marxism and of Western liberal culture, and (b) saw the respect with which Moroccan Moslems surround Allah and take the community values for granted. A. S. became a Moslem 25 years ago, and has a family with children, reverent Moslems all. He now lives in Egypt and has an Arabic name.

9. For further material and discussion, see my book *The Pagan Temptation* (Grand Rapids: Eerdmans, 1987).

ern sects, etc. It may be a paradox that the new situation, the humbling of the church through outside pressure and internal collapse, may lead to a renewed universalism and to the requirement of new methods. The adventure with liberalism was, among other things, an over-politization, meaning the church's presence in all Western debates, from Marxism to existentialism. Many have become confused about whether the church's mission is to lead souls to salvation or to form shadow cabinets in opposition to government policies.

Option B thus opens perspectives beyond itself; that is, beyond a narrowly planned shift away from the liberal West into other geo-ideological areas. The problem is not transition from liberalism to socialism, but rather this: after the almost lethal crisis that the church has undergone on the eve of its third millennium, the doctrinal continuity ought to be supported by a retreat from politics. It is now clear that the *worldly* temptation has run into a self-liquidating situation; the reconstruction, the rallying to faith, must come from the inexhaustible *divine* guidance, that of Jesus Christ. If the church remembers that it is in this world but not of it, it will be easy to liquidate, and never to renew, the various alliances. An awareness of this may arise out of the deepest vocation of the church, when it finds itself politically alone, flagellated by the powers of this world because its kingdom is not of this world.

CHAPTER FIVE

The Homeless Church

No Going Back

For the church, there can be no return to its previous historical positions. Though true of other institutions, with the Catholic church it is a different matter. Other religious bodies do actually preserve a large degree of immobility, as if they were islands hardly reacting to the surrounding turmoil. It belongs, however, to the essence of Christianity to be at all times an active participant in history and human affairs, to be plural in its approach to local and generational situations, and to promote reflection and change in science, statecraft, and culture.

The price of this theoretical and practical involvement has been a high degree of exposure to risks of internal, even doctrinal, transformations. To be precise, historical events did at times prompt official statements: encyclicals, doctrinal emphases, and other proclamations that represented by their contents the depot of faith and doctrine, the church's total truth. But the expression and timing of these were reactions to the world's momentary challenge. Of the available cases one may mention the proclamation of papal infallibility (by the first Vatican Council in 1870), which had also certainly been a practice (see St. Augustine's dictum: *Roma locuta est; causa finita est*—once Rome speaks, the matter is settled). Yet this proclamation became the explicit affirmation of authority at a time when the papacy had lost its temporal domain, the so-called papal state. One may interpret such cases as signs of supernatural wisdom and protection by the Holy Spirit, that in spite of these risks of involvement with mundane matters the church was able to resist the dilution of its essence and reassert its eternal truths.

On a larger scale, we may take as an illustration of this the transformation of the cosmological image which occurred in the last five centuries or so. As a rule, religions are anchored in a certain cosmology which they help to formulate for their believers from the beginning, or which they engender from their depth. These religions remain guarantees that the cosmic image will not be modified, that those who worship at their altars recognize implicitly a certain worldview, together with the nature and will of their god. Everything then becomes stabilized under this worldview: the image that the believers have of the structure of the universe, the place of man in nature and in the flux of events, and the interaction of the supreme will and human vocation.

Christianity is the only religion not adverse to plunging into history, and consequently not worried by sizable modifications that science, politics, and philosophy propose as genuine discoveries of the human mind. This is because Christianity—together with Judaism and to a lesser extent Islam, but more daringly and articulately than either of these other monotheistic credal systems—acknowledges a God existing outside the universe, independent of space and time, independent of mankind too, a truly transcendent being. If other religions are reluctant to scrutinize their own established cosmic image, it is because their gods (in plural) are intra-cosmic, themselves parts of the universe; they would be decisively affected, even perhaps abolished, by a new image of the cosmos. More precisely, if these religions were to integrate profane philosophy, science, art, etc., into their systems and were thus to make room for a new cosmology, this would signify from their point of view that new gods had come into existence or that old gods were rediscovered; either way, such an eventuality would invalidate the traditionally held cosmic vision. This is why these religions remain attached to their original cosmology rather than face the total upheaval of their religious presuppositions.

Christianity, on the other hand, runs no risk with a new cosmic image—for example, the shift from the pre-Copernican to that formulated by Galileo, Kepler, and Newton. The extra-mundane God never "concealed" aspects, structures, and compositions of the world he created ex nihilo; but man, with his limited comprehension, discovers them only by degrees, then adjusts his civilizational postulates to the modified image. This image holds until a new discovery—let us say Max Planck's or Einstein's—affords further or different insights into the working of gravitational and electronic forces, and into the place of the earth or the galaxy in the universe. Non-Christian civilizations, feeling "safely at home" in their cosmos, hardly encourage their experts to work on scientific discoveries, whereas Christian civilization always has. In the Christian religion there was no danger in locating new forces and cosmic events, when all eventual novelties could be subsumed under the laws of God's creation. God did not change, nor did the cosmos; only man was encouraged to discover new images and concepts and to formulate new hypotheses, trying to comprehend more completely how things actually are and how nature and history actually function. These problematics may even be called the foundation stones on which Western civilization rests.

Nevertheless, Christianity did expose itself to certain risks when, with eyes fixed on God's reassuring presence and guidance, it authorized and promoted a vast change in mankind's traditional archaic worldview. Through its very creed the Christian religion initiated a cosmic view in which archaic (pagan) religions' innumerable intermediaries and intercessionary powers between God and men were swept aside in favor of *one* such mediator, Jesus Christ, himself divine and human. To be sure, angels and saints have remained important for theology, liturgy, and iconography; but the temptation from the beginning has been to replace them, as far as the scientifically scrutinized material universe is concerned, with gravitational forces, elliptical orbits, celestial mechanics, and astral chemistry. For example, space, which was full of mystery and myth for Plato and the authors of the Old Testament, was rationally explored; humans actually stepped onto one of the celestial bodies the way Columbus stepped on the newly discovered shores of America. Among the early heroes of celestial mechanics we find not only lay scientists but Catholic priests (Nicholas of Cusa, Copernicus, Mersenne).

The transformation of modern man's cosmology—in fact, cosmological transformation was one of the chief heralds of modernity—was a symbolic act toward the removal of man from the church's traditional worldview. Voltaire understood it well when he welcomed Newton's discovery (the nature of connecting links in the universe), even though Newton himself entertained misgivings regarding his own theory, which turned God into a mere celestial clockmaker. Kant understood it too when he based his epistemology on Newtonian implications: the unknowability of things in themselves and the limits of knowledge to what categories of reason dictate.

Now for the post-conciliar church, a return to its earlier position in matters discussed in the previous chapters—liturgy, discipline, hierarchy—may be as difficult as a readjustment to the old cosmology with its sacred objects and live astral spirits. What happened at Vatican II should be seen as the last pages of a civilization permeated by Christian concepts, axioms, and a sense of reality, a sense of sacredness. It is interesting to quote for comparison the saintly patriarch Alexei, of the Russian Orthodox Church, who spoke of the murderous times of Bolshevik persecution that could not extinguish in the remaining churches the liturgy of St. Chrysostom, a liturgy which had little to do with Western forms, Catholic or Protestant. As long as the liturgy of St. Chrysostom can be celebrated, said Alexei, "our church is not in danger." The contrast with the Catholic church that emerged from the Council is enormous: the acceptance of the values of profane civilization over which the church threw its own mantle, as if it could baptize them. These values are the products of a worldview that began to be formulated in the Renaissance, and which is dominated by a cosmology that the church too tacitly adopted. The end result is desacralization, all the deeper for the Catholic church because it was not persecuted as was the Orthodox, and because in fact it contributed to its own secularization.

We must now add some details and nuances to these considerations. While there is no return to previous cosmologies, competent scientists are already modifying the strictly mechanistic character of the prevailing cosmology, one of mere traveling astral bodies in a meaningless, inexorable cosmic vacuum. A new cosmology may then be more "friendly" to religion and its sacred component. We cannot imagine how such a modification may come about, just as our archaic predecessors could not conceive in their time of our universe and the worldview it helped to formulate. One thing is sure: desacralized society, liberal and socialist, has a vested interest in the mechanical cosmology and its precision, which is mimicked by industrial society in its approach to the material world and human beings. Yet not only modern cosmology but also the omniscience and unchallenged power of modern society display signs of fragility as the dominant cosmological image, valid now for three centuries, breaks up. We are reaching the point at which we can be no more certain of the "reality value" of our worldview than were the Babylonian and Egyptian priests or the Greek philosophers. In human terms, there is no certifiable progress from the cosmic image of the Stoics to ours, and in fact a kind of stoic equanimity in morals and knowledge grows among our de-Christianized, but no longer scientifically optimistic, elites. We, like the Stoic wise men seventeen hundred years ago, seem to dangle at the end of a discredited worldview.

The exhaustion of modernity is evident in our societies. What had steadied liberalism during this century was the challenge of totalitarian regimes over against which liberalism, with its escort of humanism and democracy, was able to display its own flaws as virtues. The flaw which appeared as a virtue was the innate tendency in liberalism for unlimited radicalization, but contrasted with the radical and brutal revolution the slower rhythm of liberal gradualness made it seem like a resistance to that revolution. Already in 1918, with the course of the Bolshevik takeover from a variety of liberal parties fresh in his mind, Nikolai Berdyaev wrote that "liberals yield to revolutionaries because they are incapable of countering them with a different and higher moral truth."[1] How correct this judgment sounds in a century when the world has seen the medically performed extermination by totalitarian regimes of millions in death camps. Then it saw the same acts repeated by liberal regimes, this time in the form of mass abortions and the industrial utilization of fetuses! Berdyaev understood that liberalism was making the bed of totalitarianism and that it is bound to lie in it, even though bewilderment and anguish await it once the sham of its ideological partner is finally exposed.

Berdyaev himself was astonished at this self-betrayal of liberalism which had sheltered the radicals with its cloak of high-sounding slogans, and then accepted liquidation at the partner's hands, unable to refute those shared slogans. Why did liberalism belie its promises, the Russian religious thinker seemed to ask? He found the answer in liberal shallowness, the improbability that men of integrity and good faith would subscribe to a porous "liberal faith," a "liberal worldview." "The internal development of liberalism leads to democratic equality, a doctrine opposed to freedom; it leads to a thorough nominalism which denies ontological reality to things beyond the perceptible individual: state, nation, church."[2] Society for the liberal consists of nothing but legal relationships among social molecules. This is why in a battle between the pale liberal and the passionate social revolutionary, the revolutionary wins.

It is this absence of passion that has displaced the scene of the church's struggle in this world from liberal society to socialist regime. Liberal society seems to have closed its balance book; it concentrates now on the further cultivation of a way of life. This may be respectable but it earns no flaming loyalties since the routine has suppressed or neutralized the deeper aspirations. The price of liberal success is the nakedness of the public square where words and acts are not allowed to upset the pretense of a consensus. Religion was the first to be so

1. Nikolai Berdyaev, *De l'inégalité* (Geneva, 1976), p. 122. The book, written in Russian in 1918, was first published in 1923, in Berlin. It contains the profound analysis of factors and spiritual preparation of Bolshevism, among them the errors of liberalism and democracy.

2. Ibid., p. 128.

neutralized, made hygienic, its vocation pulled like a trouble-some tooth. The liberal project may be the better off for it, but this project opens on nothingness, on more of the same. The church has reached the point where it has nothing to do except on occasion to rush like a crazed fire brigade, putting out flames while others are lit. In other words, it behaves like liberal society itself, in decline: it makes muted affirmations of doctrine and morals, it keeps a vacuous agenda of social services, and it has an almost cynical disregard for souls in genuine need.

Under these circumstances it is hardly realistic to invite the Catholic church to occupy the center of the social stage. The true picture of the church in Western society is that of an impotent, exhausted person between two ages, wandering aimlessly in a wasteland. In other words, this is emphatically not "the Catholic moment," as Richard Neuhaus believes.[3] Granted, Americans insist on the proverbial silver lining, but not even inveterate optimists are well-advised to see what is blatantly not there. Neuhaus's thesis is that "this can and should be the moment in which the Roman Catholic Church in the United States assumes its rightful role in the culture-forming task of constructing a religiously informed public philosophy for the American experiment of ordered liberty." One may of course argue that if America actually was the scene of ordered liberty it would have an operational and effective public philosophy and would not need one, especially not from an institution neutralized by the Constitution itself. In other areas of the world, religions and churches played their leading role only if associated with the public power or when the population was thoroughly permeated by immemorial cultic realities. It is hard to imagine, as Carl Schmitt notes, that after a centuries-long association between altar and throne a new alliance can be put together between altar and office.[4] No

3. Richard John Neuhaus, *The Catholic Moment: The Paradox of the Church in the Postmodern World* (San Francisco: Harper & Row, 1987).
4. Carl Schmitt, *Roman Catholicism and Political Form*, American translation of an edition by G. L. Ulmen. The whole passage is worth quoting: "The alliance of throne and altar will not be followed by an alliance of office and altar or of factory and altar. . . . If and when economically-based power be-

public philosophy can be formulated in a modern pluralistic society except the fragile one based on sustained economic growth. And the chances are nonexistent that the artisans of economic growth might assume the responsibilities of the state and altar for the tonus of the American experiment.

Thus Richard Neuhaus's thesis would be utopian even from the point of view of the American reality because this reality, as far as the horizon is clear today, is not receptive to it. It becomes doubly utopian when Neuhaus calls upon the church to fill the vacuum with a supra-economic, public-political philosophy, religiously informed and culturally creative. Neuhaus makes a number of important points when he blames progressive Catholics for their use of the vague but fashionable term "value" instead of "truth" or "reality," and particularly for their confusion of "future" and "transcendence" (see the point made by Fr. Tischner in chapter 4). Yet he misses the all-important issue of pulling these progressivist errors into a total diagnosis of Catholic weaknesses that the church does very little to correct. Finally, his optimism is chiefly grounded in his apparent conviction that (a) what is essential is Christian unity—thus, in modern parlance, ecumenism—and that (b) this could be best achieved by the post-conciliar church which had demonstrated at the Council its remarkable flexibility in initiating a new dialogue. In other words, if we follow Neuhaus, the Roman church is or could be at the apogee of its creative powers, offering near worldwide leadership to all Christians, including Americans in their social and cultural plight.

There is in all of this a double misunderstanding. One that we just discussed is that American Catholicism will somehow be able to pull together the dropped threads of national vigor. The second misunderstanding is deeper. Neuhaus's posi-

---

comes political, i.e., if and when capitalists and workers who have come to power assume political representation with all its responsibilities . . . the Church can align itself with this new order, as it has with every order because the new sovereign authority will then be compelled to recognize a situation other than those concerned only with economy and private property" (private printing by editor), p. 20.

tion is that now is the time for the church, with half of its tradition rooted in Greek philosophy, to reassert the Aristotelean postulate that politics is an extension of ethics, and consequently to moralize America by injecting doses of Christian morality into its shabby and tattered public doctrine. But is politics really a continuation of ethics? In a sense it is: statesmen and public figures in general ought to possess a little censor in their souls which would remind them of the decency of imposing moral limits on their public actions. But this should not make us forget some political imperatives for the church that were already discussed before in some detail: for the church to be able to influence the public square, let alone to turn its presence there into a "Catholic moment," it would need public power. Let us not be so angelic as to assume that the Spirit suffices in the collective area. I suspect that Mr. Neuhaus expects the church to perform the creative cultural acts *without* possessing this ingredient, since he sees the temporal salvation of America as a consequence of ecumenism (starkly phrased, of a restated pluralism). This is not realistic, because even with "ecumenism" the church would still remain, vis-à-vis civil society, a mere interest group, a signatory of the social contract. Not until the state-church relationship is radically altered—by no means a likelihood—could the American church respond positively to Neuhaus's hopes. That, however, would be such a novel situation that we cannot evaluate it other than in abstract terms.[5]

I have left the determining factor of the whole issue to the last. A "Catholic moment" presupposes not only American and Western society's receptivity to a church-inspired public philosophy; it presupposes also the *cultic energy* of the church itself. By cultic energy I mean the absolute devotion, beyond

5. This critique of Neuhaus's thesis is independent of the fact that in America today a Catholic consensus is absolutely missing on, among other matters, elementary moral issues. The American church itself does not speak with one voice and is far from being able to take on leadership over society. Theologians, bishops, clergy, journalists, experts, and religious orders widely and anarchically disagree on all matters of faith, including New Testament morals. In fact, this anarchy is one of the factors of the American public anarchy, for which it is in no small measure responsible.

the public, the daily, and the rational, to the supernatural through all the sacramental and sacred channels. The cultic lies buried in the soil of faith, from where the church laboriously would have to extract it. Vatican II has left the cultic soil fallow and, like the industrial civilization in which the church now lives, it has re-covered it with cement. The vast bureaucracy that the Council spawned is a typically urban product—the church has joined the rural exodus. With the cultic element consequently ignored, minimized, or simply denied, the church seems to have made Karl Rahner's arrogant dictum its own: that for the church's modern interests a couple of city intellectuals have more weight than old peasant women in the dark corners of a village church. Yet without a vigorous cultic element the church may just wither away. It certainly cannot lend life to a national community's faded belief in itself.

A Soulless Society

Our discussion of whether or not there is a "Catholic moment" now in the United States brings us logically to larger areas. It is significant that after so many "Catholic centuries" the issue is at present narrowed to a "Catholic moment," as if to seize upon a (debatable) last chance of reinstilling religion in public life. This shows to what extent modern society has fashioned Catholicism in its own image and for its own purposes; it can now look at the church as one tamed instrument among many which deserves a chance of reentering the public place, perhaps through a back door.

Even more significant is the hesitation of the church between the two main forms of modern politics, liberal and socialist, a hesitation which results in the adoption of the same mixed attitude which characterizes society. The attraction is unquestionably stronger from the leftist side. The Left, or socialism, regards itself as a besieged fortress surrounded by enemies representing egoism and chaos who threaten the socialist redemption of mankind. As we have seen, the most concentrated form of a generally utopian leftism, the Marxist doctrine, looks on itself as the infallible bearer of immanent historical truth, compared to which representatives of other classes—bourgeois liberals, social democrats, progressive Christians, etc.—have been liars and wasters of humanity's substance. The passions thus generated by the Left (socialism, Marxism)—the fury at the historic injustice suffered and at the postponement of utopia—have noteworthy consequences. Radicalism, Marxism, and the various doctrines of the revolution (cultural revolution, liberation theology) engage in a far more blatantly passionate politics than partisans of liberalism, democracy, and the welfare state. The Left advertises itself as scientific and factual, and as having a concrete plan, but in reality it also exudes a quasi-religious zeal, a collective frenzy, and it cultivates a personality cult in order to mobilize energies and recruit militants—hence its success among youth and disaffected priests, as was the case at the original moment of leftism. The leaders of the French Revolution counted in their ranks a multitude of men in their early twenties and a disproportionate number of priests. In order to grasp the deep influence of socialism, wrote Gustave Le Bon, "we must understand its dogmas. Like religions whose allure it tends to adopt, socialism does not spread through reasoning and arguments, an area where it is weak. On the other hand, it is strong in the area of affirmations, daydreams, and illusory promises." Le Bon then continues: "The irrational and the passionate are more persuasive motives of human action than systems, since what masses want are hopes and faith."[6]

In the specific circumstances of our century, the leftist regimes, while advocating internationalism, equality, and the war against religion and state, act in a very different manner from these slogans and announced policies. Behind their arguments in favor of scientific methods, they stir up passion against the bourgeois state, the sham equality of opportunities offered by liberalism, the false internationalism of capital, and the patriotic facade of feudal power and privilege: that is, of banks and cartels. Ever since Marx and especially Engels, a positive tag is attached to proletarian nation, communist equal-

6. Gustave Le Bon, *Psychology of Socialism* (1986).

ity, and workers' international. In order to exalt these slogans
about a radiant future, the Left, before and after taking power,
engages in an elaborate use of symbols, as must those whose
vocation is dealing with masses and collective promises. One
of the first acts of the revolutionaries of 1789 was to distribute
red and blue cocardes (the colors of Paris) that people fastened
to their hats as a sign of opposition to the royal white, and of
course as a passionate rallying point. No need to discuss here
the part that violent colors—and music, flags, parades, watchwords, decoration, collective enthusiasm, mass rallies, charismatic persons, and, of course, bloodshed—play in every revolution. Those regimes whose justification is to perpetuate the
revolution (for example, Trotsky's and Mao's permanent revolutions) must encrust these symbols in their daily routine as
reminders that the combat for the cause does not wane.

Yet it does wane, particularly since none of the promises
is fulfilled or can be fulfilled. Thus a Marxist regime is ceaselessly led to invent enemies, imminent perils, domestic con-
spiracies, and obstinate opponents whom the entire population
must locate, pursue, punish, or eliminate. The campaigns
against must recapture some of the zeal and enthusiasm with
which the revolution had begun; in order to ensure the inten-
sity of the revived revolutionary moments, the use and reuse
of the trusted symbols is indispensable. But since the symbols
and the verbal symbols, the colors and the sounds, the hand-
clapping and the orations cover only unkept promises and
bring back memories of bitterness and disillusion, the regime
must increasingly resort to the rehabilitation of prerevolution-
ary collective loyalties and symbols. Both of these have roots
in much deeper layers of belief and experience; they elicit, as
the new slogans do not, the spontaneous manifestations of a
more genuine ground of the soul. Stalin, for example, faced
with the likelihood of losing the war against Hitler, revived the
memories, images, and charisms of Holy Mother Russia because he was aware that his soldiers would not fight for the
Soviet regime and for international socialism.

Such a gradual change of symbols brings with it a change
of underlying loyalties too. A vicious circle commences: as the

regime loses its hold on people's imaginations and their response to the ideological slogans, it is compelled by the logic of the situation (and since sheer force also spends itself) to reach down to deeper layers of loyalty, which can only be national and religious.[7] The process, a gradual one, rehabilitates the fundamental realities, until it cannot be reversed. The regime which started out with the grim intention of suppressing religion and nationhood finds that the mere task of governing requires some degree of loyalty and civic discipline, and that these in turn are only available through the tapping of traditional channels. A further trap for the regime and its official ideology is the inseparability of nation and church, since the latter had stood at the birth of nations, nurturing consciousness through the religious identity, then protecting it against threats of dissolution either by invaders or by domestic efforts to liquidate the national awareness. It is illusory to believe that these voices of tradition may be extinguished, an illusion common to socialism and liberalism. They survive time.[8]

Note that all of this does not amount to an eventual return of religion and church to full public existence, let alone to political presence and participation, to a widened "Catholic moment." From its double experience with inimical regimes and societies the church could only learn a negative historic lesson—negative when compared to the preceding two millennia, yet beneficial regarding the future. In a sense, the chastised church is compelled to retrace its steps and reemphasize its pure vocation. Its accusers have for a long time called the Roman

7. As soon as Gorbachev's "new policies" surfaced, analogous to the first setbacks of the Red Army since 1945, in many places of the Soviet empire, from Afghanistan to Esthonia, mass protests began, national and religious in character.

8. What is described here is not only the situation of the Catholic church in countries like Poland or Hungary. It is also that of other religions under communist regimes elsewhere, and of situations and movements in history. Greek national consciousness, for example, which was brutally suppressed for four hundred years under Turkish occupation, was kept alive by the Orthodox Church through the teaching of writing, catechism, literature, and music, transmitted to the population at secret meetings.

church "Constantinian," meaning that it usurped varieties of worldly powers. There is evidence to back this view: within one hundred years the church was rolled back from its advanced positions. In 1870, Vatican I registered the loss of territorial power; in 1965, Vatican II registered the liquidation of political power—if, that is, we regard the recent council as an acknowledgment of the failure of the church's presence in exalted, morally decision-making positions. It is of course tempting to hold a different view, namely, that the second Council has politicized the church even more thoroughly, only no longer on the "Right" but on the "Left." Yet the council has also matured to the truth that the path of politics, in either direction, leads nowhere, that it is rocky and sterile. The loss of alliance with the state, itself now confiscated by liberal society or by the socialist party (or by third-world military regimes), closes a long chapter in the church's temporal pilgrimage.

Essence and Form in the Church

It remains to give a more concrete answer to so many people's anguished question as to whether the church will indeed survive, and if this is taken for granted, what great transformations it will undergo. There is, I believe, no reason to assume the church's "self-demolition" (Paul VI); besides, nobody can conceive how such a thing would come to pass. In any one historical period public imagination stretches only to the limits of the known; very few are aware of the vast past upheavals of the church and the necessity to build it up again, almost from the foundation stones. The church has always lived with crises.

On the other hand, our century has been unique in the sense of being a revolutionary period par excellence, so that the church too passed through a revolution, no matter what meaning we attach to that term. But as in the past, there have been those revolutionaries who have wanted to "save the church from itself," abolish or at least diminish its transcendent essence, make it rational, scientific, and modern, stress its conformity to the world—or, to the contrary, some have demanded that it renounce the world and choose pure spirituality. One new element in the situation is that the leaders of the church have allowed authority to be diluted, and following the convictionless and permissive character of liberal society they have presided over a kind of glorified but generalized "bull session" at all levels of the church's operations.[9]

What then are the perspectives? We quoted once before St. Vincent of Lerins. Let us again accept his guidance. In his *Commonitorium* (A.D. 434), the monk of Lerins (a small island monastery off the coast of Cannes) lists three criteria for testing Christian truth: that which is believed everywhere *(ubique)*, always *(semper)*, and by all *(ab omnibus)*. These are hard to verify, and people observed in the age of navigation and exploration that at least the first and last requirements became unascertainable. The true criterion is then the second ("always"), the deposit of the faith and its authentic development, from its origins in Christ to the Last Judgment, as preserved by the apostolic tradition. It does not have to be everywhere, and it also can be preserved by a small number and not by all. Cardinal Newman has profound passages about what constitutes authentic doctrine and its formulations through ages and civilizations. He takes Vincent of Lerins as a guide. Both assert that the deposit of the faith is in the hands of the supreme magisterium, but that every correctly conducted mind is capable of judging the legitimacy or illegitimacy of doctrinal development; namely, whether the newly explicit statement is contained in the intention of the original deposit from whence it is drawn, without change or alteration.

---

9. An outstanding example of the permissive moral guidance that bishops provide is their conference's endorsement of "educational efforts, including accurate information about prophylactic devices [against AIDS] or other practices." At the bishops' meeting at Collegeville in the summer of 1988, only Bishop Eusebius Beltran (Oklahoma) dared raise his voice to ask: "Are church educators to offer instruction about how to select and employ condoms?" Mgr. Beltran continued by reaffirming the obvious, that "it is not for the church to expose people to instruction on how to disobey God's law with lessened risk to health." From a letter by Cardinal Ratzinger to Archbishop John May, president of the bishops' conference: ". . . such a proposal for 'safe sex' ignores the real cause of the problem, namely the permissiveness which . . . corrodes the moral fibre of the people."

In one sense, then, the previous questions asked about the church's future should be reformulated as one overarching question: Will the essence of Catholic teaching remain intact in spite of recently introduced variations that risk affecting the essence in the midst of new circumstances? St. Vincent had set down the framework within which the validity of the question may be stated: What was taught before should now be comprehended with a greater clarity, but in order for this to happen one should be sure to teach the same thing as before, even if in a new form. In other words, the task of the church's teaching magisterium at all times is not to say new things (new essences), but to say the same things in a language appropriate to the times. In St. Vincent's view, the development (not change from one essence to another) of an idea is its amplification, without departing from the original meaning; change occurs when the idea goes beyond itself and becomes another. It is good that faith increases and is strengthened in every Christian throughout the times, as long as it remains attached to the same dogma or doctrinal clause in the same sense and with the same sentiments *(sententia)*.

To return once more to St. Vincent's terminology, even if the essences of church doctrine remained intact, the form in which the prevailing speculative language surrounded the church rapidly produced a new style of thinking, a new framework of reference, and indeed a new doctrine. In the church too, subjective values, endless dissections, and personal judgments and sentiments became the standard of reflection and the principle underlying the action. Speaking of biblical exegesis in the past fifty years or so, Cardinal Ratzinger had this to say recently, at a convention held in New York (January 27, 1988): "Gradually, the picture became more and more confused. The various theories increased and multiplied and separated one from the other, and became a veritable fence which blocked access to the Bible for all the uninitiated. Those who were initiated, were no longer reading the Bible anyway, but were dissecting it into the various parts from which it had to have been composed."

Yet a respected theologian like Yves Congar can declare that this century is the most evangelical of church history, thus equating faith according to the gospels with a shapeless and confused "search" for the true identity of Jesus Christ, for the meaning of Christianity, for a melting down of believer and atheist into a new Christian type. As if all intellectuals inside and outside the church spoke in tongues, celebrating a new Pentecost, the meaning of words, concepts, and definitions is devalued or rather transvalued. Not only are the secular critical doctrines doing their corrosive best inside the church (the church now "open to the world"); these doctrines acquire additional radicalization through their combination with clerical zeal. Nietzsche's diagnosis proves correct: it is not only that Truth has begun to move (as in Hegel's philosophy); movement itself is now the Truth. The ordinary Catholic today is bewildered by the cafeteria-style liturgy of, for example, baptismal, nuptial, and funeral ceremonies where the priest acts according to the wishes of the family, altering words and gestures at will. The pope exhorts the bishops to preserve liturgical unity, but on returning from Rome his brothers in the episcopate choose the comfortable way out and neglect to enforce a minimum of cohesion.

These few examples of the ravages of the critical doctrines place before the church a terrible dilemma. It is not a question of the church's self-liquidation or lack of resistance to pressures. The issue for the church is to occupy a new place in the world, a place that Paul VI, a very sensitive man, summed up while he was still Mgr. Montini, archbishop of Milan, and then repeated toward the end of his pontificate: "The church will continue to open and conform itself to the world, thus to disfigure its own nature. But its supernatural substance will be preserved, limited to a residual minimum, and its supernatural end will be pursued faithfully in the world by this remnant. There corresponds to the church's false expansion as it dissolves itself in the world a gradual contraction and impoverishment in numbers. They will form a minority, seemingly insignificant and dying, but this minority contains a concentration of the elect, giving firm testimony of the faith."[10] This message

10. Romano Amerio, *Iota Unum: A Study of the Variations of the Catholic Church in the Twentieth Century* (Rome: Riccardo Ricciardi, 1985).

at the end of his pontificate, given February 18, 1976, thus concluded with the prediction, almost a secret wish, that the church be reduced to a handful of defeated.

Aside from the Gnostic tone of this otherwise deeply moving declaration (Gnostic in the sense that it distinguishes between a small group of elect and the large number of the believers who are thus sacrificed to historical determinism), the lost cause is further underlined by the pope's earlier speech (November 1969) concerning the use of Latin in liturgy. The conciliar constitution on the liturgy states in its paragraph 36 that "the use of the Latin language . . . is to be preserved in the Latin rites," but that "a wider use" may be made of the vernacular. Characteristically, Paul had this to say about the matter: "We are losing the language of the Christian centuries . . . and will lose a large part of this marvelous spiritual achievement, the Gregorian chant. . . . How are we to replace it? It is an inestimable sacrifice." Contradicting itself, the rest of the discourse argues that the people will gain by using their own everyday language.

The apocalyptic and at the same time hesitating style, not expected in a papal statement, surprises only those who see in the church's pilgrimage through history a somewhat less prosaic but nevertheless natural parallel to secular events. Montini was a tortured man, consumed with pride, yet crucifying himself at the crossroads where the clash finally took place between Christ and the world. He had an exacting spiritual idea of the church's vocation, an aspiration for asceticism, and the impulse of a limitless giving to the world from the reservoir of the church's charity, which he may have mistaken, like so many of his Catholic contemporaries, for humanism. The two impulses coexisted in this pope, and they divided him, nailing him on the cross of the immense responsibilities he felt toward the church and mankind, the two destined to meet, perhaps, he thought, in this century (close to A.D. 2000), perhaps under his pontificate. This may have been his own perception. Men less influential and lower in status than Montini also believe these times to be apocalyptic, eschatological, and their attention is fastened on this or that aspect of the decades since 1945 as the plenitude of times. Yet a pope is not allowed to project his own sensitivity and Christian agony on the wide screen of the church. His biographer and periodic interviewer, the philosopher Jean Guitton, writes that talking with Paul "one did not feel the presence of a priest but of a layman suddenly placed on the papal throne."[11] The apocalyptic mood is extremely dangerous; it shows that one man sets himself against Christ's promise and thus demoralizes, from his high position, the rest of the men and women entrusted to his pastoral care.

It remains that Montini's agony sums up and symbolizes the tribulations of the church in the modern era and points to these centuries as the road to Calvary. What are these tribulations? Simply put, the church has come dangerously close to the world, its eternally tempting alter ego. No question that the Incarnation may imply this danger, but it also provides the antidote—spirituality rather than politics. For the past two centuries, however, politization has kept edging its way toward the heart of the church; with its cold grip it would have snuffed out the church's life. This has not happened because politization in its liberal guise led too obviously to a miscarriage, to an unnatural relationship. We cannot therefore speak of an apocalypse, notwithstanding Pope Paul's sinister declaration. But the pope was right in another respect. In its contact with modernity, structured, we add, by the liberal doctrine, the Catholic church "disfigured [*dénaturer*] its nature." This sin will pursue it, since sin always attaches itself to the sinner until he is destroyed—or touched by grace, as in Dostoevsky's novels. Redemption may then come not by switching from liberalism to socialism—although this *is* now an ongoing experiment—but by withdrawing from politics and its labyrinthine corridors.

No eremitic way of life or even penitence will ensue, only the recognition of the papal diagnosis, even if not the papal remedy. True, the church is unable in the present situation to unify a fragmented world, but the supernatural substance of

11. Jean Guitton, *Paul VI secret* (The hidden pope) (Paris: Desclee De Brouwer, 1979), p. 17.

which Paul spoke can be preserved. As the church shrinks to a remnant it will no longer be tempted by mundaneness, and the world's political and cultural leaders will not find it an attractive ally.

The new course will not be charted because "small is beautiful." The church's involvement in the world is a positive thing, part of its doctrinal essence. Nor should the church be small (the terrible term "remnant" must not echo in our ears) or be restricted to one category of men; it was by divine providence that the apostles co-opted Paul, who co-opted the gentiles, who in turn co-opted the Roman empire with its vigorous millions of barbarian subjects.[12] Yet the pope spoke of a "residual minimum," the steadfast people whose weight must balance that of the many others engaged up to their necks in the illusory experience of expansion. The residual minimum is emphatically not a group of Gnostic elect, but identifiable men and women grasping the crucial moment: retreating from mundane alliances, and focusing on the supernatural vocation.

It is improbable that we shall notice the change; it will not be announced the way the Council was announced among applause and intrigue as a new beginning. It is certain, however, that a kind of unwinding is necessary, a slowing down of the panting speed with which the church for several centuries has accompanied mundane movements and transactions. In the eyes of many, the deceleration seems out of the question. Our image of the church (which Rome fostered) is that of a full participant, an "expert in humanity" (Paul VI), not because it knows human nature, which is evident, but because it wants to be present in every human endeavor. This was not really the church speaking in a genuinely Christian tongue. It was the world's language, spoken by a church dizzy with its own superman's pretensions, a language that Rome unconsciously made its own. Theology too adopted this worldly, self-promot-

12. A detailed and well-documented study about how the church became the guide and protector of post-Roman Italy (6th to 9th centuries) is provided by T. S. Brown, *Gentlemen and Officers: Imperial Administration and Aristocratic Power in Byzantine Italy, 554-800* (London: British School at Rome, 1984).

ing attitude, desirous to baptize the various philosophies of progress. It declared first that since man is God's cocreator there can be no science which would not sing God's praise, no technical innovation escaping God's approving attention.

Its second claim was that history is revelation in its forward march, a kind of immanent providence. This view authorized the Hegelian, then the Marxian, theologians to play with the theme of dressing providence and revelation in more worldly garbs. The consequence of these theological considerations, long before the theology of progress or of liberation had been heard of, was the christening not only of science and technology and whatever they were going to produce, but also of history and the future (Teilhard de Chardin is the most spectacular representative). In short, together with liberals, progressives, socialists, and Marxists, Catholic theologians in good standing declared that everything that is modern is good, and that the contrary notion smacks of Manichaeism or outright pessimism. Thus the church, at least a strong and vocal sector of it, espoused modern thought together with the modern world. It is hard to blame the world for not feeling guilty; it was told to assume the posture of Prometheus, unbound by the Christian Zeus. What I am saying is that for centuries the church underemphasized its mission of proposing its own view of the world and man to a world in increasing disarray. Chances are that the church did so for tactical reasons. How could it reasonably oppose modernity, which was rushing in with youthful enthusiasm: democracy, industry, free press, an abundance of goods, nations founded on consensus and contract. It was as difficult to point out the dangers of social anarchy and technological dehumanization as it is today to warn against youth culture, abortion, pornography, or idolized human rights. Nevertheless, the church's task should have been to press relentlessly for an alternative to immanence (stark this-worldliness), and to the glorification of man and his achievements. Instead, the church too allowed itself to be caught up in the religion of unilateral and simplified progress, and manifested its satisfaction when occasionally the world asked for its blessing and approval. Gradually, the "this-sided-ness" of modernity proved contagious; the church went along. It would have been in bad taste to criticize or block it.

But of course immanence was not innocence. It was pulling the world into shreds through the proliferation of critical doctrines: free thought, individualism, systematic criticism, all with a darkly negative side. On the one hand, it was the organized exercise of reason, on the other a battering ram—like Diderot's Encyclopedia, Lessing's plays, Condorcet's progress of humankind, Bentham's strict utilitarianism, etc.—directed against all institutions and social and spiritual realities. It has ever since been argued that such a legion of enlightened thinkers would have tolerated no opposition from the church, which they regarded as their chief enemy. Countering them with the Catholic worldview in the public place would have been an impressive, historic achievement. Instead of this, the Roman response was ad hoc and sporadic: the *Syllabus of Errors* (1864), the first Vatican Council's proclamation of papal infallibility (1870), the first social encyclical, *Rerum Novarum* (1891), and *Pascendi* against modernism (1907) were strong and wise statements; but they seemed to be mere reactions to the modernist theses which followed each other in an ever quicker succession. The impression gained ground that Rome—its thinkers and scholars—was unable to produce original art, literature, political theory, or philosophy. The conclusion was that, seven hundred years before, Thomas Aquinas was able to do original work by adapting Aristotelian philosophy to Christian doctrine; and before him, Augustine adapted Plato. But, it was held, by the nineteenth and twentieth centuries Christianity had become ossified and could not create anything original of its own (neo-Thomism was believed to be a rehash of rigid scholasticism); nor could Christianity latch on to science, producing Christian interpretations of such modern systems as those of Darwin, Marx, or Freud.

The Effects of Vatican II

All this is not mentioned here as an overview of past lacunae or as a suggestion that the church somehow missed a chance to build its own "counterculture." It is mentioned as a response to Pope Paul's *cri de coeur* about the church "disfiguring its nature" and the "self-dissolution" which follows on a "false expansion." What is listed here are symptoms on which the papal diagnosis was finally made—namely, that by the end of the last century the critical doctrines established their preponderance, then virtual domination, unchecked. No wonder that in the last thirty years, since Vatican II, the church has become a veritable ancilla of civil society's culture, hardly able to protect the Catholic elite and masses against it. While rising with a sure and competent judgment and concise language against the various outgrowths of modernism (encyclical on Marxism in 1935; the *Monitum* against Teilhard de Chardin's teaching, 1962; the encyclical *Humanae Vitae* in 1968; the *Instruction* on biogenetic manipulation in 1987), the church still failed to inspire anything like the Thomist synthesis or to formulate a public philosophy beyond a permutation of the clichés of the day. The Second Vatican Council which was expected to turn its attention precisely to these tasks—this had been the declared intention of Pius XII and John XXIII—announced itself instead as a "pastoral" gathering, which was a way of falling in with the spirit of the "social question" and its prescribed conclusion. It was a way of telling the world that the church too, until then, had behaved in a lordly, arrogant manner, not listening to the poor abandoned by both society and religion. This was emphatically not true, but the church was so embarrassed by not having taken the highway to progress that it wanted to correct the impression the world allegedly entertained. The symbolic act of atonement before society came when Paul VI deposed the papal tiara and approved (we saw with what agony) the elimination, from then on, of Latin and the Gregorian chant in the liturgy.

The secular translation of these acts equated the church with capitalism in the process of yielding to economic reforms, a false parallel and a groundless apology. In this manner a golden opportunity was missed. The Council could have declared that the causes of misery, discrimination, and modern wars were to be sought in the situations created by the postu-

lates of social science, misapplied technology, excessive industrialization, the evacuation of land, and the massing of the
population in urban areas. Yet these things remained shame-
facedly unsaid so as not to put in question the premises on
which progress rested. Thus the conciliar deliberations set out
not to save men's souls but to illustrate material and social
concern, and they became filled with a verbose and pointless
parliamentary rhetoric. By calling itself "pastoral," the Council
on the one hand neglected the aspects for which it had competence: the morals as taught by Christianity and the true
doctrine on which they are founded. On the other hand, it took
up, with a servile enthusiasm for the fashionable discourse,
those aspects which fall outside its purview: other religions,
pluralist societies, human rights, and the government's obliga-
tions to accommodate a multiplicity of faiths.

In essence, the Council debated Catholics' adjustment to
the liberal mores. The adjective "pastoral" came to mean not
the pastor's charity for the flock ("You have not chosen me, but
I have chosen you"—Jn. 15:16); instead, it was used as an
umbrella term for the clergy to find fault with the ecclesiastical
structure, particularly with the aspects of it relating to discipline, celibacy, the wearing of cassock and habit, democracy
in parish and diocese, and the like. "Pastoral" also acquired a
meaning vis-à-vis the laity. Its men and women were now
described as people "come of age," competent to pick and
choose their own diet of religiosity, mature enough to "live their
faith" as they understand and approve it. Thus the pastoral
concern unmasked its real intention: to elaborate a magna
charta, and even more concretely a declaration of indepen-
dence.

The Council was then indeed a watershed, but not in the
way it is semiofficially regarded: as a mere up-dating, a kind of
dividing line between the traditional and the modern church,
between old obedience and new freedom. Rather, it was a
culminating point of the church's all-too-deep involvement
with this world, with the experiment of making a Christian
society by placing the responsibility for it on mere human
shoulders—Maritain's program. *Christian humanism* was a

hybrid expression, intended since the Renaissance to adjust the two sides of human nature to each other without friction. Since the nineteenth century the term has been further loaded with the task of producing a Christian humanistic society, by definition also without conflict. Jacques Maritain claimed to have found it in the United States, his disciple Pope Paul in the Council and what it prefigured. Fr. John Courtney Murray is our witness that America, after all, does not qualify as a Christian humanistic society, but rather as a secular humanistic one; and we are witnesses that the Council did not bring forth a Christian society either; its good intentions merely helped to pave the road for the scandals, blasphemies, and breakdowns of the last three decades. The "liberal" Council reproduced the contradictions of liberal society, contradictions between the claim to be free and the results of anarchy and disunity. Yet there is a difference between liberal society and the liberal post-conciliar church. The former, in Berdyaev's diagnosis, evolves toward democratic egalitarianism by its own inherent logic, and because of this inclines to its opposite and loses its freedom.[13] Since, to continue with Berdyaev's reasoning, liberalism is basically nominalistic, it denies the genuine ensembles, corporations, institutions, states, nations, and churches. Thus there is no philosophical contradiction when liberal society turns into its opposite, the egalitarian society, where no authority but only brutal force may prevail. Exit liberal society. But the church cannot become "liberal" and dissolve authority, institutions, structures, and discipline. Their absence or even weakness threatens the souls Christ entrusted to the church. Liberal civil society—a "halfway house," as Christopher Dawson called it—turns into something else. It never possessed the deposit of the faith; it was only the storage place of philosophies which may be rejuvenated and tried elsewhere. If not in New York, then in Singapore or Tokyo. A liberal Catholic church, on the other hand, is a nonviable contradiction, a kind of class struggle,

13. "The state exists not in order to turn worldly existence into a paradise, but to prevent it from becoming hell." *De l'inégalité*, p. 58.

with members believing different things and parishes acting on different moral premises. Once this happens the church cannot be reconstituted "elsewhere." Paul VI was right: even if with only a residual minimum, continuity must be sought in the pursuit of the supernatural end.

There are potent, even urgent reasons why the church should turn to the business of spirituality. True, it has never abandoned it, not even in the present dark days. Accompanying the excesses of this-worldliness and politization there are constant and magnificent testimonies of intact and nourishing faith and of the works of reason inspired by it. If numbers were important in this respect, one could cite instances that are deeply satisfying, which indeed exemplify the true miracle: communion with Jesus Christ. Yet even though they are caused by a minority, the scandals and the signs of indifference are not only too many; they are of such a nature that publicity gets hold of them and uses them to devastate the faith and sense of decency of millions. A true measure of the low level to which the church has allowed itself to be degraded in modern society is the free-for-all mockery and blasphemy of Jesus Christ in books, movies, plays, classrooms, round-table discussions, television, and the press. Here is a true measure not only of a misguided toleration on the part of the church, but also of the place it now occupies in the hierarchy of social institutions. Mohammed, Moses, or Buddha would not be treated in the shameless manner in which it now seems normal to treat Jesus. Society seems to say to the church: Just try to talk back, try to defend yourself! We know how to silence you and to remind you of the contract you signed; you have no choice but to submit!

This may be a modern form of Christ's continuing re-crucifixion, and others suffer with him an undeserved agony. Many of the crucifiers are inside the church, so millions of believers lose faith, suspecting that the church lacks the courage to fight back. It plays by the liberal rules. This "cultural" exploitation of Christ by satanic people who hide behind the liberal dogma of "freedom of speech and artistic creation" is not a mere spontaneous endeavor but a direct consequence of the affirmations and ambiguities of Vatican II. Its "pastoral" character was correctly interpreted by the church's adversaries: it meant that the church is weak and dares not, perhaps cannot, proclaim the faith or the wisdom which comes from it. It did not dare proclaim Augustine's *credo ut intelligam* (faith leads to understanding) for fear of ridicule by the prelates' academic colleagues. It is safer for the church to hide behind concessions of internal democratic reorganization and external pluralistic good relations, safer to accommodate one's neighbor rather than follow Jesus' words: "If you were of the world, the world would love its own; but because you are not of the world, but I chose you out of the world, therefore the world hates you" (Jn. 15:19).

A combination of outside circumstances and the impasse of the liberal church will compel it to retire to its own spiritual vocation, the only nourishing source. In this respect, Paul VI, who contributed so much to the crisis, will prove right about the "impoverishment into a small number" who are the concentrates of the faith. Let us reflect upon the shape of imminent things.

CHAPTER SIX

On the Pilgrim's Path

The title of this chapter may be understood in two ways, and, as we shall see, they are not contradictory. The church has always been on the path of the voyager (the medieval theological term is *viator*), and good ecclesiology interpreted that path as a never terminated pilgrimage for men through the tests and trials of earthly existence, until death. The temptation, expressed in the misuse of the term *ecclesia triumphans*, always was to claim that the church summed up history, or rather that sacred history is achieving victory over the parallel, secular events; it pulls ahead of them, so to speak. If anything, this century's vast tribulations have proven that in history "triumph" is always precarious, never definitive—it cannot be taken for granted. In these pages we have seen the church as signatory of a contract or as petitioner, as an object of derision and persecution, and finally as an almost negligible quantity vis-à-vis civil society or the totalitarian party.

But even discounting events of recent centuries, we can say from the larger perspective of *Heilsgeschichte* that the church is a pilgrim who never knows what providence has in its plans for her and who is not quite sure how her sins are weighed on the divine scale. The use of the fashionable term covering all Christians, "people of God," does not change matters; its implied flattery and elevation to a pedestal have no echo either in God's judgment or in history. People of God today, a chastized community tomorrow—chastized through an excessive immersion in secular concerns which we called politization.

The second meaning of the expression "pilgrim's path" is the great and perhaps not yet fully evaluated lesson of events around us as they affect the church as an ongoing institution. In spite of the widespread belief—indeed, the ideological center of the times—that church, state, and society have finally reached a consensus, a practicable modus vivendi, and that each has found its own groove allowing no return or even deviation, we have shown that this belief is factually erroneous and morally fraudulent. The church is now—as we look at it at one given moment of the secular side of its history, a dramatic moment—more seriously threatened than at any moment of its past. Simply put, its path *must* now diverge from that of the world, the one bearing the tag of secular, liberal, industrial society. Whether liberal or socialist, industrial and technological society has a fatal bent toward gigantism, and with it dehumanization. As Christopher Dawson phrased it in speaking of Western culture, it is impossible to go farther down the road of secularism which has been followed for so long, because this road has reached its ultimate station. Only two alternatives remain. We can either set up abode in the "half-way house of liberal democracy, striving desperately to maintain the higher standards of economic life which are the main justification of our secularized culture; or we can return to the tradition on which Europe was founded and set about the immense task of the restoration of Christian cultures."[1]

We agree with Dawson that liberal democracy is a halfway house, and would only add that the road leads to a kind of totalitarian mix of secular state and secular society, whether the community of robots calls itself "revolutionary," "socialist," "modern," or what have you. We disagree with Dawson, however, when he envisages as plausible the alternative of restoring Europe (or the West) to Christian culture. Every element of such a restoration is lacking, partly because the

1. Christopher Dawson, *Christianity in East and West* (La Salle, Ill.: Sherwood Sugden, 1981), p. 87. (My italics.) Dawson's warning is identical to the critical tendency of modernity (liberalism, science, technology, robotization) which runs through the work of Henri Bergson, José Ortega, T. S. Eliot, Berdyaev, Ellul, A. Gehlen, etc.

"triangular equilibrium" mentioned earlier—of state, society, and church—has been completely disavowed and liquidated.

The hope is lit elsewhere. The obvious danger is that the church too remains trapped in the liberal-democratic halfway house as a contracted agency that is not to embark on anything beyond the dos and don'ts of the contract. But the course of the church is not determined by the desperate bent for growth of industrial society. "Growth" and "industry" have no meaning in religion because the church is not a secular society based on success in economics, expansion, military status, or human rights.[2] It does not fit into a category. And in spite of the ideological blockages of certain of its members, some of them blocked in the expectation of the apocalypse, others in the expectation of utopia, the church itself is a free agent in history because it belongs to two histories, the sacred and the profane. It can change tracks, pursuing both or only one history while holding onto the other.

Just as there are stations on the pilgrim's progress, so there are stages in church history. Industrial society with its ideological product, liberalism, was one such stage; disengagement from industrial society and its ideology very likely will be the next. The Western world, dominated by science, technology, and liberal morals, cannot jump the rails. It is turning before our eyes into a mission territory, already morally a wasteland, with only the technological frame holding it together. But technology may serve Marxist societies too. In fact, according to one variant of the modern myth, Marxism promotes large groupings, collective ownership, and super-bureaucratic management. The issue of liberal society turning socialist has nothing to do with the efficiency motive; the transfer is effected on the moral plane of beliefs and myths. It

2. The obsession with expansion at any price has inflated to include the multiplication of human rights. "Contemporary liberalism," writes Fr. Francis Canavan, "is so intellectually and psychologically invested in the doctrine of ever-expanding rights—the rights of privacy, the rights of children, the rights of criminals, the rights of pornographers, the rights of everyone to everything—that any suggestion of the baleful consequences of that doctrine appears to them as a threat to the liberal idea itself" (*Catholic Eye*, Sept. 15, 1988).

seems that the two forms subsumed under industrialization, consumership, and egalitarianism are going to perform innumerable steps in the forward-backward dance within the Western impasse; the church risks losing its soul by participation in this catatonia. At any rate, it cannot interrupt or modify it. Just as Roman culture was one of statecraft and the following centuries lived under a Christian culture, the overarching civilizational idea of the modern West should be known as economics. Christianity was able to link up with, and permeate, a culture based on statecraft (with its two pillars, law and architecture) because culture had a transcendent opening. The *Aeneid* is a myth engendered by statecraft, the notion of the imperium; the *Divine Comedy* celebrates the Christian drama of perdition-to-salvation; but nobody writes a culturally pivotal epic poem about economics and industrial growth. Catholicism has no hold on them, nor is it of any deep interest among them.[3]

How the Kingdom Comes

It appears, however, that at this stage of its pilgrimage the church is also incapable of offering *beliefs* and *heroes* (the stuff of imagination and myth) to surrounding society, because God in our civilization has become a non-hero, a tolerated and secondary hypothesis toward solutions of the world enigma. God is not "dead" as was claimed some twenty years ago; he is only incurably distant, so distant that an impersonal, mechanical clockwork in his place is more credible today. A corollary of this scientific myth is what Joseph Ratzinger suggested in a recent speech to Chile's bishops. The idea, the cardinal said, that "all religions are mere symbols of the big Incomprehensible is gaining ground in theology and liturgy." Forget for the moment that the Vatican itself contributes to this idea with such spectaculars as the Assisi gathering; the fact is, as

---

3. Michael Novak's "theology of capitalism" is a derailment of Catholic doctrine, symmetrical to that other derailment, "liberation (or socialist) theology."

Ratzinger pointed out, that faith cannot grow under these circumstances because "faith really consists in my commitment to the truth so far as it is known." The Incomprehensible blocks any such attempt.

The Ratzinger speech reminds us, however, of St. Paul's speech to the intellectuals of Athens who also worshiped at the altar of the Unknown God,[4] and to whom the apostle brought the message of the living flesh-and-blood Christ resurrected from death to save all men. The Athenian philosophers did not become converts, but the message stood its ground; the episode symbolizes the church's present position. Paul preached to the gentiles, which is also the task of the church now. It presupposes the opposite of what Emile Poulat diagnosed. As we saw in chapter 2, Poulat believes that our age is that of the universalization of Christianity through its gradual accommodation with modernity. Not only Christianity, but all religions would be absorbed in this brew, with the result of producing a syncretistic "spiritualization" of mankind, present and future. We know that such expectations were also entertained by some personalities of dying paganism, beginning with the fourth century, who, defeated by the new religion, were hoping for the sporadic survival of pagan philosophical (stoical and neo-platonic) elements within the church. In other words, such expectations and calculations are symptoms of civilizations in agony, not signs of a commitment to faith, belief, and heroes.

All this does not mean that we should equate the Athens of Paul with an almost romanticized third world as a mission territory par excellence. It was argued in previous chapters that the third world is "occupied," solidly occupied, by religious blocks sturdier today than the Christian insertion in Western society. The new stage of the pilgrimage is, in a sense, "nowhere," unless we count, as we should of course, all the implantations of Christianity practically everywhere. It is, however, a question neither of new initiatives nor of a pursuit of what is already there; it is a question of the spirit.

4. Its contemporary degraded duplication is the rock (a meteorite?) placed in the "meditation room" of the United Nations building.

The overwhelming problem of many areas of the world is what natives and foreigners call "modernization," by which they mean the imitation of industrial society. At that level religion cannot play any role, since it would lead again to politization, taking sides, forming shadow cabinets, and finally whispering in the ears of the powerful—the well-known cycle repeated on other shores.

The church possesses other resources, independent of location and responding to the soul's needs. One cannot define and plan for them in advance; they emerge from concrete situations. The church is not an enterprise of human engineering. What impresses people everywhere, and in many instances "turns them around"? Service that nobody else is willing to provide and that cannot be duplicated by mere human means. This is up to the heroes that the church still abundantly raises up, persons inspired in their actions by the extreme originality of Christ's own deeds. The God-man scorned in the West is still an astounding figure elsewhere. He is *believed*, together with dogma, moral teaching, and the gospel story—none of it rationalized, subjected to hermeneutics, or simply denied. In short, Christianity is believed by vast numbers of men and women not in spite of the doctrine but because of it. Service as it is here understood is not a washed-out philanthropy, nor is it a set of humanitarian acts wrenched from Catholic doctrine and made to navigate on their own as "problems" to be solved through social concern. Much is said these days about the principle of subsidiarity which is at the heart of Catholic social thought and many papal encyclicals. It is the principle which suggests that the lower rungs of collective bodies such as a society, a nation—a corporation of any sort, from the family up—should take care of matters within their competence, leaving all else to the immediately higher rungs. This principle is often spoken about in a spirit alien to it, namely, as a response to the welfare state and its insistence on planning and bureaucratizing the simplest issues.

This is a secondary consideration. Stripped of rhetoric, subsidiarity means what common sense dictates: people should be placed in a position, materially and mentally, where they can fend for themselves. For this to happen, dedicated men and women are always available. There are Mother Teresas in larger numbers than is assumed, and, like Mother Teresa, they perform their duties to fellowmen out of love of God. Asked about why she cares for the most miserable wretches of Calcutta—the starving, the abandoned, the old, the exposed babies, the terminally sick—this woman answered that from a strictly human point of view one is repelled by the work of locating, washing, caring for, feeding, and comforting the lepers and other wasted creatures; it is done because God commands it to be done for the littlest of his children. The same answer was given to American researchers investigating the motives of those who were saving, hiding, and otherwise protecting Jews during the Second World War. A Dutch Catholic, identified only as Dirk, said this: "I did not save Jews because I have an altruistic personality [the researchers' assumption and thesis] but because I am a Christian who obeys Christ. The Lord wanted us to save these people, so we did."[5] In other words, not because of horizontal philanthropy but because of vertical obedience to the Father. When Catholic newspapers—for example, the diocesan paper, *La Croix*, of the Parisian episcopate—orate about the church's "necessary insertion in society, its necessary closeness to the people of today," the first and last words give away the sociological preoccupation, the cold approach, since "insertion" takes for granted society's primacy, with the Christian religion as an afterthought, and "today" directs us again to a sociological entity, the product of circumstances which we do not really wish to change.[6]

It is thus evident that Mother Teresa, the Dutchman Dirk, or Maximilian Kolbe, none of whom knew anything about "insertion in society," could not operate without Catholic doc-

5. Samuel and Pearl Oliner, *The Altruistic Personality: Rescuers of Jews in Nazi Europe* (New York: Free Press, 1988).

6. *La Croix*, 2 July 1988; the paper mentions this social insertion together with the other "musts": religious freedom, ecumenism, human rights, in other words the litany of updated ecclesiastical stereotypes. This hard-eyed, not-at-all veiled warning shows that charity is far removed from this social program.

trine, which Mother Teresa almost incidentally summed up in the foregoing quotation. "Father" does not mean an anonymous agency or a world body with a budget to spend by the time next year's grant is allocated. My experience of witnessing missionaries at work, nameless ones unlike Mother Teresa, made me understand the nature of the link between such work and doctrine, a link generally underestimated in today's nakedly activistic worldview. Words like *generosity, help, concern, improvement, commitment,* and *love* mean hardly anything unless the missionary is known by those who rely on him to have sacrificed his life for the work he has undertaken. This is the case of the people mentioned above and of countless others. I met young priests from the United States in the high plateaus of Bolivia ministering to people and sharing their life in a desolate and dreadful place; German nuns in the jungles of Africa, who had taught young black girls for forty years; Dutch priests in Taiwan caring for mentally handicapped local children abandoned by their mothers. All of these are convinced that they have become trusted and followed because people around them know they will never backtrack, leave, give up, or despair. The notion of "lifelong" is the key to genuineness. In the event that these servants are recalled by Rome or by the Order to which they belong, natives will understand, aware that charity includes discipline and that there must be superior reasons, independent of the missionary's will. They are reassured that the same discipline and charity that they have come to trust will send them someone else who is also ready to sacrifice his life.

In these considerations we have not really left the principle of subsidiarity. The missionary and those around him form, after all, a family, a group structured on its model. All power is essentially a domestic power, structured after the home; every leader is first a father. Modern political science denies it, but real life reaffirms it at every turn. The missionary is thus perceived as a father (psychoanalysts ridicule and degrade the term when they speak of a "father figure") with an extended family. Parish and community are born together, the link forged by God, man, and circumstances. There are dangers. Men and women working in such sacrificial situations run into the temptation of letting themselves be absorbed in the human dimension of their tasks, neglecting the supernatural dimension. Through the persuasive action of *pride* they come to perceive the environment they created as their own work, which may continue on its own logic. God's work is forgotten as the main ingredient. This happened with the worker-priests in the 1950s who were absorbed by labor unions and who gave the mission to themselves, as it were, instead of receiving it from God. This signalled a complete attitude change: the source of what began as a dedication to God came to be seen as the labor union and ultimately as the communist party behind the syndicate. The scope of work was modified into the building of the Perfect Society along Marxian lines. The worker-priests soon left the sacerdotal vocation and became labor union organizers with political interests in mind, without concern for the workers.[7]

The same thing may be said of the liberation theologians and the priests who follow them. The original intention may have been attachment to the church and a correct understanding of the nature of social commitment through *its* teaching and presence. Then pride advised a different course: a self-created spiritual milieu. They grew impatient with God's slow penetration, done, after all, through human means. Therefore, through resistance, imperfections, and fallbacks, enthusiasm cooled. Marxism offered a shortcut with immediate, spectacular results, then fame and martyr status, the false hero's rewards. The final phase is ecclesiastics taking up the gun and serving regimes that persecute Christians.

In both cases, that of worker-priests in France and liberation theologians and guerrilla priests in South America and the Philippines, the deviation and radicalization came about be-

7. Simone Weil's example is significant insofar as this Jewish girl in the 1930s, in soul and mind a Catholic, saw through this hypocrisy. An astoundingly perspicacious intellectual, Simone Weil went to work in factories so as to understand and share the condition of workers. From close experience she realized that Marxism is not the answer; it too exploits the workers, often by exacerbating a bad situation and thus prompting a revolutionary attitude.

cause of an insufficient understanding of Catholic doctrine. God and man work together; man should not take over. This is no pious statement; it means that forces above man must be allowed to work themselves out—concretely, to let habits change with time, sink in, make room for themselves. Obviously, Marxism dictates a different course; its logic and sense of time are products of the demonic, forged in "dark satanic mills." They demand—with brutal methods—rapid action, direct means, and efficacy, and carry inhuman consequences. But there is a "Marxism" in every age, the way of radical this-worldliness. The reminder is therefore always necessary, and it must be an institutional reminder.

Doctrine and institution are necessary because all men have a clear consciousness of their sinning nature. The church cannot enter on its missionary vocation with only a haphazard goodwill that would presuppose sinless human beings, as modernity sees them. We argued in the previous chapters that modern man and the clumsily self-modernizing church are caught in the web of this presupposition. No matter how widespread an attitude this is, in the confrontation of the individual man with reality his personal doorway is forced ajar. The philosopher and the missionary interpret this openness differently. The first, often infected by the sociological viewpoint and methods, envisages large categories of people—intellectuals, professionals, workers, women, the young—and undertakes to measure their reaction to faith. I have Karl Rahner particularly in mind because he held that man's essence is openness to transcendence in such a way that God is actualized in the soul—he is the author of our actions. If this were so, we would indeed not need an institutional church; people would find their own salvation. But this view of sin and salvation is also marked by impatience. Those who follow it rush ahead and interpret their actions as manifestations of divine closeness, divine inspiration. Over against sociological heaviness which scrutinizes unwieldy ensembles, Rahner's existentialist optimism cheapens access to transcendence. Perhaps the explanation is that the German Jesuit was more interested in fellow intellectuals than in average people, and intellectuals notoriously believe that God or an oracle, history or class, race or the future speak through them.

The missionary's center of gravity is elsewhere. He deals with individuals of a more modest rank than Rahner's; his work teaches him to organize his categories not according to an occupational directory but according to need, suffering, unexpressed movements of the soul: miseries of all sorts. He deals with ordinary sinners whose desire for redemption is *also* fed by their material wretchedness. The contemporary form of utmost dejection, the refugee condition, offers pertinent examples of the naked cry from the depth of despair. Whether boat people from Indochina or Ethiopian peasants driven off their land, the misery in the eyes of the destitute shows even in the hyped pictures of sensationalistic reportage. These eyes express more than material want. They express a suffering which calls for redemption. At such a state of animality body and soul ought to be lifted up together. As Mother Teresa says, even death is accepted in exchange for a few days' or hours' status as God's child on whom charity shines.

These situations of want are what missionaries deal with, "missionary" here meaning the spiritual understanding of the church's central vocation, one it must take up again. It is a theology of mission rather than liberation. It should be obvious that we do not speak only of the missionary phenomenon as such, but also of the church's permanent *mission* redeemed from worldliness. This is part of the need for periodic purification which, contrary to its promise, the Second Vatican Council did not effect; it only made the need for purification more urgent and thorough. Cardinal Ratzinger recently said:

> After the Council there were many priests who deliberately raised "desacralization" to the level of a program, on the plea that the New Testament abolished the cult of the Temple . . . on the plea that religion, if it has any being at all, must have it in the non-sacredness of daily life. . . . Inspired by such reasoning, they put aside the sacred vestment; they have despoiled the churches of that splendor which brings to mind the sacred; and they reduced the liturgy to the language and gestures of ordinary

life, by means of greetings, common signs of friendship, and such things. . . . We ought to get back the dimension of the sacred in the liturgy (and the essential in the liturgy is the mystery!). The liturgy is not a festivity; it is not a meeting for the purpose of having a good time. It is of no importance that the parish priest has cudgelled his brains to come up with suggestive ideas or imaginative novelties.

And so on and on, as the highest official of the Curia expresses himself about a council that called itself "pastoral."

The point here is not only the liturgy and the issues Ratzinger mentions. Quoting him is useful for our discussion of the missionary church. What the cardinal describes here shows precisely the incredible impoverishment of the missionary spirit. Under the pretense of sacralizing the whole world and every aspect of daily life, the post-conciliar *ecclesia* allowed itself to desacralize religion itself, displaying in these acts an avaricious spirit, in stark contrast to a much-advertised generosity. Avaricious not only in what Ratzinger calls the despoiling of the churches and liturgy of their beauty and mystery, but also in the sense of depriving people—not the intellectuals but the average believer—of charity, of reliable presence, and even of a decent milieu for worship. For decades we have witnessed a turning away from the missionary understanding of the church's task, and a consequent turning toward a purely cerebral, cold, sociological approach.

This does not mean that political tasks ought to be excluded from the next phase of the church's pilgrimage. Politics is inscribed in human nature; its denial leads, within the church too, to anarchy and utopia, the two poles of unrealism. Politics enters in the new situation through the fact that even charity organizes itself, becomes an institution, creates networks. The Cluny revival in the tenth century spawned three hundred monasteries in a few decades, and contributed to the strengthening and spread of religious fervor, learning, music, and architecture. "Spiritual politics" would be, nevertheless, an ill-sounding term, and I use it here only as an available alternative to the overinvolvement in the business of societies, political systems, and regimes which has locked the church in a dead-end street. Politics, in other words, can be built up simply from the church's presence, a presence no longer loaded down by problems of "political interests," which concretely in the United States means tax-exempt status, the camouflaging of religion at supposedly Catholic universities, the mini-doctrine of the "seamless garment" which shelves the issue of abortion until all issues of extinguishing life, like wars and capital punishment, are also abolished.

Challenge for the Western Church

The road that now opens for the missionary church is certainly not new. Those who from the beginning penetrated all areas of northern Europe and the Near East, and before then Africa, the peripheries of Asia, and the Americas, traveled it. Today it is the same road and yet not the same. The Christian penetration used to transform these areas and continents, always finding receptive people and states of mind because the teachings of Christianity set into motion beliefs, thoughts, impulses, and behavior not satisfied by other religions. This was not only the Christian concept of charity, but, just as important, the doctrine. Why is doctrine the ultimate argument even when Christianity is carried to simple laborers and peasants, people ignorant of the Hebrew and Hellenic traditions, rural or city folk fearful of the impact of foreign ideas? Why does doctrine lay the true foundations of belief and charity? Reduced to its essential minimum, Christianity brings to people the God-man, mediator between a sinning creature and a loving God; it also brings the dogma of salvation and redemption, able to call forth an earth-moving élan in all areas, from spirituality and mysticism to material achievement. Under the severely formative impact of most other religions, and certainly the polytheistic ones, it is everywhere believed that the human being is a plaything of cosmic forces which are unapproachable except by sacrifice (tribute) to their representatives, the manifestations of nature. But the personalized spirits lack moral dimensions, and their indifference—very often cruelty—stamps human relations too.[8] The personal God of Christianity is not only a moral being; through incarnation he is also one who suffered, died, and resurrected. In other words, he united in his life on earth the human condition with divine understanding and forgiveness. Even when fears of ancestral demons and despotic divinities survive in the soul of certain populations, in their legends, art, and literature, the impact of Christ creates at least a parallel, and often an overcoming, loyalty.

Ecumenism does not enter the picture at all; it is a game that intellectuals play with a political arrière-pensée. Polytheistic religions are extremely demanding, with their multitude of cultic figures, spirits, demons, powers, and influences crowding in on worshipers day and night. Worshipers live in fear, trying to propitiate the deities with constant gifts and through meticulous formulas and gestures. Any deviation from them brings instant retaliation or a delay of fright and wondering anguish. The rewards too either depend on the god's whim or are automatic payment for a large tribute and a meticulously performed magical act. The Christian religion (and Islam too, particularly in Black Africa) brings a relief from these oppressive forms; it brings forth the moral understanding latent in all people, underlined by a personal God who is father of all.

Wherever the church might turn in the next decades— and the emphasis on missionary tasks in the non-Western world is both obligation and necessity—it will not relinquish its efforts in the West, near the place of its origin and foundation. We spoke before of the West as a mission territory, and this was no figure of speech. We also mentioned that liberal democracy, built on the premise of a limitless increase of human rights, rights of consumership, leisure, and moral

8. For Sankara, the main interpreter of the Hindu Vedas (eighth century A.D.), creation evaporates before the undifferentiated purity of Brahman (world spirit). Neither love nor the knowledge of God is possible. Hindu wisdom denies reality and calls it an illusion (maya). The Hindu religious teacher demands absolute personal loyalty, in contrast to the Catholic missionary who communes in the common faith with the soul he guides. He is a mediator between God and man.

emancipation, is the most fragile construct in the history of human achievements. It may not outlive this century. The end may be neither a bang nor a whimper, but, less spectacularly, either surfeit or a drying up of the Faustian impulse. Whatever the unwinding of our civilizational cycle may bring, it will present religion with new opportunities.

A Call to Spirituality

New challenges are facing Catholicism then. No longer—or at least less and less—is the challenge the political one of survival in self-idolatrous societies; instead the challenge is that of spiritual presence. The Western crisis is of such a magnitude that other religions are flooding the Western heartland, and reflective people have begun a mass exodus from Christianity, converting to Buddhism, Hinduism, Islam, and varieties of occultism. Some take this as a good sign, in the direction of their desired coalescence of all religions into one supersystem; others see in it a welcome exchange between religion and society, a universal and mutual accommodation in which religions are absorbed, leaving behind them a vague ethical flavor. These proposed solutions of the crisis are, however, part of the crisis itself, the liquidation of religion as a spiritual and sacred source for the soul.

The benefit derived from spiritual contact with other religions is indirect. It reminds the church that religion is the most serious business for men and that one's own cannot be sold for a political mess of red pottage. This realization will help the church in the coming enormous task of reconcentrating upon itself like a drowning man who, with a last soul-wrenching effort, pushes up to the surface. The rest of the story cannot be predicted, such as changes in structure or liturgy. Yet it seems reasonably certain that extremism and politically inspired radicalism will not have in the future their present, quasi-privileged places that were the products of recent alliances.[9] As these

---

9. It is worth noting that while Rome had no objection to bishop-statesmen like Cardinals Cisneros (around 1500) and Richelieu (around 1630),

alliances lose their raison d'être—mainly because society's interest in the church diminishes—theological and liturgical radicalism will wither away like unripe fruit falling from branches extended too far. Even with regard to excesses half-approved by the Council or implicit in its decrees, the trend now, a generation later, is toward rescinding them and returning to a state of equilibrium. When Cardinal Ratzinger calls mystery "the essential in the liturgy" (see pp. 140-41) or says that the Council was not a "super-dogma which could take away the importance of the rest," the rug is pulled out from under the new doctors, the Hans Küngs and Rosemary Ruethers.

Option C (if I may add another lettered option) ought to consist of respiritualization at the expense of politics.[10] The area of activity opening up now is large, not only geographically, but more importantly, in the moral sense. This is not a gratuitous program. Two principal aspects merit examination.

(1) When power in the Western world was shared by Christ and Caesar, the relationship between the two was, in spite of the well-known and numerous conflicts, one of mutual accommodation. The centuries were in many respects brutal, and the twin powers behaved accordingly. Nevertheless, the basic assumptions were the same and this consensus spread over the entire society, giving it a moral content: all agreed that no society may survive without a moral substratum which cannot be divided into a multitude of group moralities. When Vatican II proclaimed, in *Dignitatis Humanae*, that nations must accept, even promote, religious plurality—which also

---

it forbade the political involvements of such priests as Miguel d'Escoto (foreign minister of Nicaragua's Marxist regime) and Joseph Drinan, S.J., ex-congressman from Massachusetts. The first two may have been regarded as protecting the church's teachings and interests, the others as being inimical to them.

10. It should be evident by now that I do not regard politics as something evil, degrading, or ignoble. Yet I think that a line of separation exists between the *ecclesia* and those immersed in the labyrinthine interests and methods of politics. The separation of state and church was a historic catastrophe; now it is time to reap its unexpected benefit: a sincere inner detachment on the part of the church. We have reached anyway the bottom of iniquity when among the bishops of the United States only a handful can be found who protested bodily against abortion and submitted to arrest. Christ would have called the others pharisees covering themselves with the cloak of the "law of the land."

brings with it moral plurality—the final blow was administered to the unique form of authority that had prevailed for millennia under the leadership of palace and temple.

While the church's moral teaching has remained the same, "Caesar" has assumed many identities, each with different ideological consequences. In the last hundred years or so, the state in turn has been a bureaucratic apparatus, a utopian project, a welfare organization, a popular sovereignty, a one-party rule, a military junta, a *Rechtsstaat,* and so on. Not only administratively but also from the angle of moral content, the palace has at times radically changed. The question on people's minds is whether the church will also pursue a course different from that of the past, whether it too will propose variations: instead of the moral steadfastness, a pluralist morality. This would of course be a self-destructive operation, a kind of last word in the process of imitating liberal civil society. The logic of the contract signed with society would be nakedly displayed for what it is: a blockage of Catholic faith. *Dignitatis Humanae* appears to be just such a blockage. Pluralism may be inevitable for "melting pot" communities where the citizens' religious and moral postulates were shaped by their groups of origin—a heritage that each brought with him on joining—but it is self-defeating in communities which each have a different, homogenous tradition defining their very identity. It would be even more contradictory in the case of the church which cannot subscribe to a "situation ethics," a relativization of morality on the collective scale. That would be preaching one morality while winking to others following a different one.

Such blockages—let us call them limit situations labeled *non possumus*—awaken the church to the one true universality: teaching and standing up for the same doctrine in season and out of season. Until now this was not blatantly in question, since the church was anchored in the West which has preserved, or so it seemed until recently, a residual Christianity and Christian morality.[11] But as the church feels compelled

11. We may call "residual Christianity" the beliefs and attitudes of nineteenth-century liberals whose inner world was no longer Christian but

spiritually to leave the West and undertake a new apostolate in the wider world, as it is squeezed out of the West by an anti-spiritual and anti-moral religion—secular humanism—its integrity demands a more monolithic, nonpluralist missionary message. It will not do to accept all the moral attitudes it meets; the church is only respected if it is always and everywhere the same, if its unity is doctrinal, liturgical, and moral.[12] Alas, that unity is no longer linguistic either, an immense loss deplored but not remedied by Paul VI.

(2) Until these times, the many centuries' conflict centering on the duality of power in the West, between Christ and Caesar, seemed to be the most significant controversy. Modern experience instructs us that this duality was not as deep as we were accustomed to believe, because the relationship of spiritual and temporal powers used to bring face-to-face fundamentally compatible elements; all power comes from God. That controversy, that duality, is now dwarfed by another, hitherto envisaged only as a temptation: the controversy between the spirit and the world. The reason is that in the past the temptation of losing oneself to the world appeared to be an individual matter, the model for which had been provided by

---

who still inherited enough of it to behave decently and function in their milieu according to these norms. These norms were, all told, a practicable mixture of Christianity and classical humanism, a philosophy of moderation and respect for higher things. School curricula and professional codes also reflected these norms so that the general tone of life was civilized, displaying high values.

12. There are and have always been exceptions, many of them necessary, some overzealously accepted. Adaptation to local conditions is a double-edged weapon: on the one hand, it is not good behaviorally to uproot people; on the other hand people do expect different things from daily life and spiritual life, or the life of the faith. In the present anxiousness to adapt the church to everyone, the clergy often goes overboard in flattery, which turns out to be a sign of contempt. For example, African Catholics complain that liturgy and architecture, among other things, are exaggeratedly "africanized," a fact which excludes them from Christian unity. Catholics of India bitterly complain that their bishops and clergy adapt to Hindu ways, not only as patriots, which is understandable, but also in religious and ceremonial matters. Doctrinal unorthodoxy is then not far off. They know, perhaps better than the occasional Roman visitor, the perils of Hinduist religious influence, and were upset when a priestess of Shiva put Shiva's sign upon the pope's forehead during his visit to India.

Satan's temptation of Christ. Now, however, entire societies, even the state and the church, may suffer from a loss of moral conscience. Mundanity attacks on all fronts. It represents a public-political weight, pulling us downward against the upward pull of grace.[13] Vatican II made the error of attempting to bring God and world so near each other as to fuse. It is of course evident that the church is called to stand by the world and love it, both its saints and its sinners; but as Chesterton ingeniously phrased it, love requires two distinct persons: if I fuse with my fellowman, I cannot love him.

This warning against love understood as fusion[14] is addressed to the church for the first time in its history and points to the fact that it has absorbed dangerous doses of modern ideology. Yet the ideological world poses unacceptable conditions: the church today does not face mere individuals immersed in the world, but naked worldliness itself—worldliness become policy and more, worldliness become religion. Over against the many panaceas (inspired incidentally by the world as its ultimate cunning), spirituality must not only be reasserted; it must be raised, so to speak, to the level of counterpolicy.[15] This is the first requirement, and John Paul's great merit is that he has understood it. His travels and ceremonial visits, even with their at times clumsy aspects—when the pull of old politics becomes apparent through the prayer

13. See Simone Weil's great writing, *La Pesanteur et la Grâce*, with an introduction by the Catholic philosopher Gustave Thibon (Paris: Librairie Plon, 1948).

14. Plato's view of beauty, love, and wisdom is apposite here. One of the myths that his spokesman tells in the *Symposium* clarifies the relationship between the one who possesses beauty and the one who does not. It is the one who lacks it who appreciates it (the ugly, the poor, the deficient), because possessing it would make him complete. Not the rich but the penurious know the value of wealth.

15. This idea was brought home to me in a letter from a friend who was arrested, with dozens of others, for protesting at the entrance of an abortorium. While they were facing counter-manifestants, whose features were distorted with hatred and death threat, the police officers escorting my friend and his group to jail had tears in their eyes. When laws and policies reach an absolutely abject state, disobedience is a duty—and ought to be made into a systematic counter-policy.

and the exhortation—turn faith into feast in the middle of the workaday existence through the moral confidence his presence inspires. If the pope confesses his faith and devotion in terms so commonsensical as to put the intellectuals to shame, then— the crowd tells itself silently—the turnaround of the soul *is* possible. We are not alone, and the world is not only material misery ludicrously combined with material glitter.

Spirituality will be the old and tested weapon as the church enters another millennium and lifts anchor. It will find new competitors: not political ideologies and regimes, but other religions. Just as class warfare is quieting down at the end of this century (this explains the fading of Marxism), the world is witnessing the forewarning of future conflicts: wider clashes underneath the still noisy ideologies. The clashes will probably occur between racial and religious blocs, with collisions world-wide. What emerges is not a peaceful planet, but one with gigantic forces in confrontation. The church has a built-in advantage; it is not tied, and will be less tied every day, to races, nations, and interest groups. Islam is to a large extent Arabic;[16] Hinduism is mostly of India; the expansion of Buddhism covers east and southeast Asia. Assuming that Catholicism is not tied in a similar manner to the white race, it alone possesses mobility and universality. The Moslem world will always conduct holy wars; we now see the passive Buddhist bonzes lead mass protests in Burma; and even the world-denying Hindu priesthood becomes nationalistic. The Catholic religion has a unique position. It alone is able to combine the purest spirituality and mysticism with material and organizational objectives (see an earlier passage about the institutionalized charity for the "poor among us").

It needs emphasizing that when we speak of a new spiritual and moral focus for the church, we do not have in mind a rebirth, a second birth, a sudden illumination, or the appearance of a papal guru to preside over the rediscovery of

16. Although African blacks embrace it in increasingly large numbers too. The Iraq-Iran conflict is a clash between two races rather than between the Sunnite and Shiite branches of Islam.

Jesus Christ. This kind of demagogy—another example is the promise of a "new, post-conciliar" church—represents the greatest danger. The church possesses the vocation and the ways for missionary action at all times, no matter what the century or the circumstances. In the spirit which reaches from Vincent of Lerins to John Henry Newman, development—the explication of what doctrine contains—stands in contrast to process theology, the work of the enthusiasts of a day. All that the church has to do in the dawning era is to become more clearly conscious of the bankruptcy of the West we have known and of the parallel emergence of a planet-wide non-West bearing new potentials in its entrails, for good and evil. In a way it is a replay of the centuries that followed Rome's decline and of the road opened toward "barbarian" Europe. The difference between the two inviting opportunities, however, is this: The church in the sixth century had valid reasons to remain grateful to the empire. When the empire associated Christianity to government, it reasserted with originality the lesson of history, then left to the church a model of administration ready to be used for the spiritual mission. But from partnership with Western liberal civil society the church has received only humiliation for its faith and peril to its moral teaching. Even as far as administrative methods are concerned, a danger is that the church will be emptied of its religious content for the sake of efficiency (see chapter 1, first paragraph) and become a business corporation, a super-bureaucracy, a *nomenklatura*, a machine geared to "social change."[17]

The recently deceased French Jewish scholar and publicist, Raymond Aron, summed up the tragedy that befell Europe and the West. As a tradition-respecting liberal, Aron's diagnosis carries weight. A vague skepticism has corroded the conscience of Europeans, Aron wrote, since the decline of tran-

---

17. Pastor Richard John Neuhaus has interesting things to say about the growth of ecclesiastical bureaucracy in the United States during the last decades. He speaks of the change of purpose to which these bureaucracies are now devoted. Evangelization has declined; politization and social reformism are the priorities. ("The Church of Your Political Choice," *National Review*, September 1988.)

scendental religions, and then also of secular religions, liberalism, humanism, Marxism. He links this fading of faith with the disappearance of a sense of historical mission and trust in a meaningful future. Faith and a confidence in destiny always go together; history and religion are inseparable partners. But let us repeat that the church is not a continent, a race, or a nation; its faith is not tied to historical tribulations, to a civilization's anguish over its fate. The repudiation of transcendent religion throws society into an abyss; it does not alter the character of religion and its supernatural roots.

Many new hardships await the church. For a number of reasons its missionary action may become increasingly difficult. One of these difficulties should be located right at the source, in the same conciliar document already mentioned, *Dignitatis Humanae,* and its questionably ecumenical stipulation that weakens and discredits proselytization. The falsely inspired enthusiasm of Vatican II led to the belief that converting members of other religions to Catholicism is a kind of neocolonialist and imperialist act that ought to be suspended or moderated in the post-conciliar, assumably reconciled, world. Those who preach this new approach may lack the charity they think they are practicing, since from the Catholic point of view withholding conversion from a willing candidate is a grave sin. In many instances the candidate for conversion forces the hand of reluctant priests.

The other difficulty that will arise follows from the increased contact with other religions. Since 1945, and with a big leap since the Council, the ecclesiastical personnel has become gradually indigenized, with the ordination of local clergy and the consecration of local bishops. These men are often looked upon with suspicion by their compatriots because they are perceived, like it or not, as representatives of a foreign power. It is obvious that in some instances they cannot proselytize locally. Native Catholic priests in India, for example, looking like any other Hindu of the Brahmanic caste, yet mixing with low-caste people or outcastes (harijans), are reluctant to conduct dialogues with their Hindu compatriots.

A third problem arises, deeper than the first two. When Catholicism faces other, long-established religions, it faces nominal equals. No question that Judaism and Hinduism, for example, regard themselves as superior to Christianity—the first as more ethical, the second as more spiritual—and that Hinduism emphasizes this feeling because it does not have, as Judaism does, a common heritage with Christianity. Yet, it is appropriate to take the rapport with Hinduism as typical of the rejection that the church will mostly find, because the Brahamic religion is the opposite of what Christianity teaches. It does not have the sense of personhood found in the Christian focus on incarnation, the God-createdness of the individual soul, echoed by the many meeting points with Greek philosophy.[18]

Yet, as Fr. Monchanin told his missionary students, the majority of Catholic priests must be chosen from the native populations, close in spirit both to the little people, including the despised pariah, and, through their learning, to the intellectuals. Only with such an approach, he adds, can the future Hindu St. Augustines be expected to arise from an environment so spiritually different. And not only great theologians and philosophers, but also monasteries (Monchanin himself founded an *ashram*) as places of refuge for beggars and the poor in spirit, and of artistic inspiration hopefully bursting out in Indo-Christian artforms, a fusion of the flowing rhythms of India and Christian symbolism.

Is the church now, exhausted and suffocating in the

18. Fr. Monchanin, who spent decades in India as a missionary and studied Hindu spirituality, writes that when the Greek wants to go beyond the world of senses, he passes on to the intelligible world, that of the intellect and the spirit; the Hindu first lives the world of senses, then proceeds to de-sensibilize it, tear it away from the normal conditions of experience. The de-sensibilized "object" is no longer usable, can no longer be subjected to analysis: it becomes an object of contemplation, increasingly internalized and stylized. Monchanin quotes Parmenides: "One cannot compel being not to be." Hinduism answers: Unless being was an illusion (maya) all along. Compare also Greek and Hindu art, which, however, met once in an interesting combination: after the conquest of Iran, Afghanistan, and Punjab by Alexander the Great. (For some of these comparisons, see Thomas Molnar, *Twin Powers: Politics and the Sacred* [Grand Rapids: Eerdmans, 1988].)

desacralized and neo-pagan Western milieu, in a position to take these suggestions, not only in India, but in various places and forms of confrontation with other societies and religions? The answer is yes, because these challenges are not new; they were present at the beginning in Jerusalem and Antioch, in Athens when Paul addressed the doubting philosophers, in Rome where Peter was crucified, in Africa and in northern Europe, and finally everywhere in the world. The only *new thing* on the pilgrims' road has been the experience with the self-desacralizing liberal West. This has been the only occasion when religious persecution took the deadly, subtle form of dissolution, a process which rallied not only the church's traditional enemies, but also legions of enthusiastic ecclesiastics, the doubting and doubtful elements within. It will take a long time to settle this matter, and the settlement may only have an effect with the simultaneous revalorization of the spiritual message. Then, and perhaps only on this condition, will the ecclesiastical *nomenklatura* change—or fall away. It is difficult to imagine equivocating bishops, others saluting with the communist raised fist, or still others flashing the television smile joining the ranks of saints, martyrs, and loyal believers. Yet for God nothing is impossible.

CHAPTER SEVEN

The Church and
the Redemption of Culture

The usual topic discussed by writers under a heading such as this is "Christianity and civilization"; they leave the subject of church and culture mostly to specialists, who can document ecclesiastical patronage of art, music, and architecture. Such an approach does not suit our study, in which we have suggested all along that, unless we wish to speak of the past, a Christian culture no longer exists. The writings devoted to Christianity and culture—such as T. S. Eliot's *Notes Towards the Definition of Culture* or Josef Pieper's *Leisure, the Basis of Culture*—even though they envisage a restoration, remain mostly nostalgic echoes of past achievements and imaginary projections of past conditions into the future. To repeat, there is no Christian culture today in the West. To declare the need for its restoration is a praiseworthy but unrealistic attempt, reserved usually for nostalgic groups engaged in the melancholy game of mutual encouragement.

The latest presence of the church in culture has left a dismal taste in the mouths of decent people. As Cardinal Ratzinger alluded in the previous chapter, following the Council and for years thereafter priests serving parish churches and cathedrals either threw out on the street, or, with a better financial instinct, sold the inestimably valuable art objects which had been there for centuries. A walk into many neighborhood antique stores in European cities in the 1960s and 1970s could bring to the owner of a well-filled purse freshly discarded ornate prie-dieu, episcopal thrones, tabernacles of precious wood and metal, carved wood benches, ciboria with inset stones, priestly vestments, and of course paintings and sculptures of great beauty, antiquity, and value.

Why was the church's sacred property thrown out of its home as if in disgust and contempt?[1] Ratzinger speaks of the misguided belief that the Council recommended the sacralization of everyday life, and thereby authorized the desacralization of the church itself. This is too gently put because, after all, the fury with which the operation "let's get rid of art" was conducted puts to shame past iconoclastic movements and can only be compared with the devastation of church buildings and monasteries by the Protestant reformers of the sixteenth century. But this time it was done by Catholic priests—so to speak ex officio.

Both the iconoclasts of Constantinople in the eighth and ninth centuries and the reformers in the sixteenth had doctrinal reasons for destroying sacred art. Post–Vatican II Catholic rebels also put forward arguments they claim come from church history. The religious sacred, they hold, was abolished with the destruction of the Jewish temple, symbolically by Christ, materially by the Romans. Christ was crucified *extra muros*, in a neutral place, not in the sacred city; the cult was therefore also displaced from the temple (church) to daily life. The sacred left the church with its idolatrous objects, and has found a home among the people. Its genuine presence manifests itself in love and spontaneity, not in institutions and ceremonies which are nothing but brutal concentrations of power, arrogance, and abuse.[2]

All of this indicates that the contemporary iconoclastic wave was not prompted by a misunderstanding of the Coun-

1. The irony of the situation in a country like France is that, since the anti-church laws of 1905—most of them not really enforced but still on the books—church buildings and their contents belong to the state. Strictly speaking, the object removed or sold by the curate was not the church's to dispose of.

2. Dostoevsky's "demons" in *The Possessed* engage in basically the same reasoning during the first conversation between two atheists, Stavroguin and Shatov. They justify the revolutionary destruction that the Russian writer called "nihilist."

cil's directives, nor by some silly personal initiative. After all, the elimination of Latin (church Latin, the church's sacred language) and of the Gregorian chant was the decision of official Rome, in spite of some equivocation about who wanted what and to what extent. To simplify the issue, we are correct in concluding that, in addition to a doctrinal aberration, the cause of iconoclasm and contempt of beauty is found in the surrounding taste of industrial society which has penetrated the church.[3] It happened with a greater speed and against less resistance than, let us say, when Gothic style replaced Romanesque some eight centuries ago. That change was made for the sake of a yet greater beauty and expression of fervor, a deeper penetration of light and splendor in the church building than the fortress-like Romanesque had permitted. The preference of the industrial era, on the other hand, was mainly puritanical in motivation, truly iconoclastic insofar as the Puritan, embarrassed by the reactions that sensory beauty calls forth, looks for some utilitarian justification for the presence of art. He is most of all apprehensive of mere beauty, to him something gratuitous and so unapproved by God, whom the puritanical mentality casts in the role of a stern work-supervisor. The art that industrial society produced around the 1920s and 1930s— a trend pursued till today—was resolutely, even savagely anti-decoration and -ornamentation; it included such names as Adolph Loos, Mies van der Rohe, the Bauhaus style, Le Corbusier and his machine habitats, and Lucio Costa and Oscar Niemeyer, builders of dreary and unhuman Brasilia. This art and architecture were strictly utilitarian and functional, con-

---

3. We may indeed speak of doctrinal aberration because the whole issue turns around the concept of *mediation*, central to Christianity and other religions. The sacraments and the priests are mediators between God and the worshipers, and so is, in a more modest measure, the splendor of art, as the Council of Trent made very clear. It is therefore not a coincidence that in the post–Vatican II decades both church art and the role of priests were questioned and weakened. Members of the clergy were proud of their "worldliness." They discarded vestments, the wearing of cassocks, and, logically, the objects of the cult. Artistically worked altars were replaced by ordinary tables, degrading songs were played at Mass, and priests made sermons on revolutionary causes.

sisting of straight lines, cement, steel, glass, prefabricated slabs, and cube-shaped rooms and buildings.

Such was the invading spirit, producing the appropriate style. The church had nothing to oppose it, although it once invented, formulated, promoted, and carried out the great artistic styles of previous centuries: the Romanesque, the Gothic, the Renaissance, and the Baroque. Not only did it not oppose this styleless style which was anti-Catholic in inspiration and anti-beauty in its philosophy and execution; the church, in fact, *adopted* the puritanical conception of art, adopted it fast and clumsily, with the same submissive and breathless speed it brought at the same time to other "clauses" of the contract signed with civil society. In other words, we are not dealing with vague ideas of shaping cultures or of reviving them, but with observations in the last three decades about the repudiation by the church not merely of a style, but, behind the style, of Catholic habits of thinking, one might say dogma.

What has thus happened is in stark contrast with what had happened at the Council of Trent (mid-sixteenth century), called together in response to the Reformation. Trent made it clear after the wide-ranging demolition of sacramental beauty in the northern half of Europe that art must be restored and rehabilitated in all its splendor. A sufficient reason was beauty itself, a magnificent way to glorify God, but beauty also makes it easier for the worshipers to understand doctrine through the senses. This, after all, refers to incarnation, the Christian rehabilitation of matter and the senses which had been repudiated by much of Greek philosophy from Plato to Plotinus, and by the Gnostics. Vatican II, which was widely understood to be a counter-Tridentine gathering, did not proclaim guidelines for the role of art in the church—a strange oversight from a "pastoral" Council—but by not retaining Latin and the Gregorian chant it signaled to the aggiornamentists its willingness to jettison beauty together with other manifestations of tradition. The new zealots in dioceses, parishes, and bureaucracies seized the neo-iconoclastic spirit that trickled down to their levels.

We may surmise that many of them felt regret, as did

parishioners with a decent taste; yet the renewalist slogans urged compliance with the conciliar mentality because here was the opportunity to update the whole church by creating an environment stripped of beauty, splendor, awe, and mystery.[4] These things all of a sudden were considered the main enemies, the four horses of the Apocalypse; their elimination came to be regarded as the magic solution for the sociological problem of bringing back to the church the workers, the young, and the intellectuals. In reality, the stripping of the church, like abstractionist undertakings in general, is a measure taken not in favor of but in opposition to the interests and preferences of believers who need and love beautiful religious surroundings. Yet starkness was equated with a more direct face-to-face encounter between believer and Christ, and was artistically interpreted as producing something suitably simple, a neutral milieu, the blockhaus style replacing religious splendor and solemnity and blending submissively with the industrial imperatives.

While it is easy to understand that a certain style dominates every age, it should be pointed out that in the past religion usually dictated the canons of architectural beauty. When the pharaoh built the pyramids, it was for an eternal resting place, a huge mortuary chamber in which all the religious symbolism was present; the Parthenon was a temple to the goddess Athena; and the greatest artists vied for parts in the construction of the dome of Saint Peter's. The novelty is that now civil society dictates the architectural changes, and the cultural ones in general, from which the sacred style is entirely excluded. The office building is now the sacred edifice that the Gothic cathedral used to be; this shift is startlingly symbolized by New York's St. Patrick Cathedral, squeezed among and dwarfed by the surrounding "feudal" fortresses of Rockefeller Center, where the cult of business has its headquarters. Society

---

4. Before the Council, many Americans became converts partly for these reasons—namely, the presence in church and liturgy of those elements they were missing in their materialistic daily lives and in their pre-conversion places of worship.

has constructed a counterstyle, part of the counterculture; the church submits to its own desacralization through the architecture it chooses, thus implicitly acknowledging its marginalization. As usual, the ecclesiastical zeal surpasses the expected. In some places, the Catholic style of centuries is blatantly defied by the architects that the church commissions. One example is the cement cube in Burgos, on one shore of the Ebro river across from one of the most beautiful Gothic cathedrals of Europe, with an insane and frightening Christ dangling from wire. Another example is the cathedral of Brasilia, the new capital of Brazil, where originally a cement ecumenical tent had been envisaged by its architects; it later became the cathedral—nothing more, in reality, than a kind of huge underground ramp with plastic chairs placed randomly here and there by the worshipers and the curious. There is also a hardly perceptible altar table "somewhere," since the interior of the cathedral has neither shape nor focus. This garage-like construct and the cinema-like church in Burgos are adequate and significant indications, with thousands of others that we cannot list, of the determined will to desacralize religion in *all* its aspects. Cinema-church, factory-church, supermarket-church, playground-church—these are now the standards for an institution which used to inspire and order the great creations of the Gothic and the Baroque.

Admittedly, a culture is not only its architecture, although the search for and public expression of beauty are best manifested in architectural styles. But there are other signs too of the separation of church and culture that no one may have envisaged or foreseen at the time of the separation of church and state. As long as the church was a *public* institution in alliance with the state, a certain standard of nobility and magnificence was natural to maintain. Popes, bishops, and abbots were in many cases great patrons of art, commissioning artists, discussing with them, influencing them, and insisting that their own taste should be integrated with the resulting work of art. The product was usually a happy interaction. Memorable are the violent quarrels between Pope Julius II and Michelangelo, the pope threatening to have the painter thrown down from the scaffolding (on which he was painting the ceiling of the Sistine Chapel in an awfully cramped position) unless he finished his work by the date set by the pope; and the Florentine master daring His Holiness to carry out his threat before he, Michelangelo, decided that he himself was fully satisfied with the work. In our age, when the church has allowed itself to be privatized, then hushed when it raises its voice—in our age of timid, bureaucratic, and puritanical taste—such a thunderous quarrel between pope and artist seems inconceivable and contrary to the rules—perhaps contrary even to Michelangelo's human rights. Yet what the violent words truly reveal is deep devotion to beauty; for both pope and painter beauty is intimately linked with faith and adoration. A huge anthology could be filled with illustrations of church patronage of art; and indeed, better than an anthology, a great book was written by Chateaubriand, published under the title *Le Génie du christianisme* (1802), the thesis being that all art in the past one thousand years and more had been Christian, inspired and sponsored by churchmen. The book was also the first post-revolutionary answer to the Enlightenment with its flat, unpoetic style, excessive rationalism, and repudiation of the past. Next to civic sponsorship of art— under the pharaohs, the Persian kings, Pericles, Augustus, the Khmer kings, the Moslem khalifs, the Medicis, etc.—church patronage brought to life the greatest talents: Suger, Bramante, El Greco, Goya, and many others.

Yet culture is more than this. It is not one particular order of activity of a community or an age, but a total embrace, permeating space, time, mentalities, and aspirations. In essence, culture is not something tangible like a Greek statue, or audible like a Beethoven sonata; it is a *hierarchical order* of all the manifestations of a given time or society, the highest organizing principle of an ensemble. Our civil societies are deaf to such intangibles; they are incapable and unwilling to create a hierarchical order—first, because they do not believe in ensembles, only in individuals. And second, in their view freedom is defined as uninhibited spontaneity. The impact of liberal society on culture lasted as long as it did because it inherited from the Christian centuries an artistic and generally cultural judgment of deep insight and balanced proportions. This heritage incorporated norms which, however, belonged to a harmonious combination of Christian drama and classical measure, and which faded out under the one-dimensional materialism we have now installed as the ruling criterion. But materialism and utilitarianism are destructive of anything noble and superior, and their first attack is directed against the very notions of order and hierarchy. The cultural consequence is obvious: since the new culture, built up by civil society and intolerant of other influences, acknowledges no distinction between good and evil, beauty and nondescriptness, decency and obscenity, suitability and disharmony—everything becomes a matter of individual taste, whim, indifference—there can be neither good taste nor correct judgment in matters of culture. We witness the pileup of junk in museums and exhibits, see the jarring disproportion of buildings which line the streets, and hear ear-shattering noise claiming to be music. A recent panel in New York, discussing "absolute values in art," could not agree on anything more fundamental than "some like it, some don't." But it was scandalized to hear from an outsider that art has, first of all, a great deal to do with sources of the sacred. The panelists would have preferred to settle on some "consensus" as the norm, presumably the product of a voting procedure yielding a temporary majority. (Why are such panels organized, money spent, participants mobilized, when they are aware from the start that certain conclusions are forbidden, certain notions outlawed, some views anathemized, all of it in the name of a free debate about culture?)[5]

5. The quality of culture in modern industrial society shows the poverty of creativeness (although the word is profusely used), and the other phenomena that accompany fallow periods. The industrial-productive mentality multiplies objects without distinguishing among them. Our museums are, accordingly, storehouses of "objects" accumulated as if in fear that no great artists will come afterwards; in truly creative ages there is no such desire to make inventories and pile everything in a kind of glorified storage. On the other hand, showing the poverty of imagination and consequent envy, beautiful sites are mutilated with ugly afterthoughts, such as the monstrous glass pyramid built in the center of the Louvre in Paris, distorting the entire landscape and

The error of otherwise profound critics like Dawson, Pieper, Eliot, and others is to imagine that norms of culture may be restored by a correct diagnosis of the ills, then by the decision to give effect to such a diagnosis through some appropriate remedies. There are no planned and consciously devised remedies, a statement well supported when we consider that culture, in whole or in detail, was never restored, duplicated, or transplanted, and that no great culture was ever foreseen, planned, or prepared. T. S. Eliot adumbrated this when he wrote about the fading of Christian faith, the proximate cause of the fading of European culture: "Then you must start painfully again and you cannot put on a new culture ready-made. You must wait for the grass to grow to feed the sheep to give the wool out of which your new coat will be made. You must live through many centuries of barbarism. We should not live to see the new culture, nor would our great-great-great grandchildren. And if we did, not one of us would be happy in it."[6]

A wise vision, not only because it acquiesces to the nature of things and the passing of time, which impose a long perspective, but also because it makes us grasp the fact that the new culture would not be a replay of the old, but something not yet experienced, something to which we could not attune ourselves, even though it may be glorious and fulfilling. Standing under their domes and mosaics (the iconoclastic fury long over), citizens of tenth-century Constantinople would have regarded as baffling the first Gothic churches (end of the twelfth century) with their ogival shapes, long colored windows, buttresses, and statuary, even though both styles, Byzantine and northern French, were products of the Christian spirit and had their roots in the same sacred.[7]

---

an admirable perspective. It is as if the present, unable to attain an independent status in the light of beauty, would choose a parasitic existence on the achievements of the past.

6. T. S. Eliot, *Notes Towards the Definition of Culture* (New York: Harcourt Brace Jovanovich, 1948), p. 122.

7. The roots were the same, but the branches very soon diverged, a state of affairs sealed by the Great Schism of 1054. The Greek Fathers differed from the

Yet, there are continuities and other elements which explain how culture comes into existence. The word *culture* contains *cult*. Art and religious history teach that the presence of culture is inseparable from that of cult. They converge because both require faith in the supernatural and total dedication to it, which gives artistic creation and religious belief a platform above contingencies. The true reality is inaccessible to human beings burdened by the senses, but because man *is* a sensory creature his highest satisfaction is derived from expressing the inaccessible through the senses. This greatest of all paradoxes typifies human beings and compels them to produce symbols which, when polished and suitably elaborated, become artworks. This is also what Plato's myth so clearly implied (see chapter 6)—man, who lacks the ideal, reaches for it ceaselessly because he knows that it exists in a world of which he can be at best a temporary citizen. But the moment of possession—for the mystic, the artist, the worshiper—is filled with the whole of reality. The rest of the time he merely remembers it and works out compromises; in rare moments it is a fusion.

Still, this domain of individual experience would have nothing to do with culture—a *collective* motive and achievement—if there did not exist somewhere a grasp of reality so potent that it imposes itself on a community and an age. Such a grasp cannot be anything but religious, and it comes from the church's grasp of the supernatural. What the church thus created was neither the accumulated and well-used riches nor the Renaissance popes' taste, but its own overarching dogmatic formulations: absolute trust in Christ, the Holy Spirit, and the saints. The Credo, the Nicene Creed, contains the art of many centuries. Its mysteries inspired Meister Eckart's sermons, the "smiling Christ" of Moissac (a church in France), and the science of Nicholas of Cusa. Michelangelo's private universe was a room in that infinitely grand mansion of the faith. What he painted on the walls and vault of the Sistine Chapel were

---

Latin Fathers in some assumptions regarding the relationship between God and Christ, in the apophatic tradition (God is too distant to be named), and in the consequent enlargement of Christ as a "pantocrator," a kind of emperor in heaven.

glimpses of the eternal spectacle, a spectacle seen and shared by others rooted in the cult of the church.

The real question about culture today then is this: Has the church lost its mediational function—between the supernatural and the soul, and so between beauty and art, between a noble outlook and culture? Has it ceased believing in the faith that formed it—with the immediate consequence that artists feel a void they cannot fill with their personal ideologies? Not only artists, but the entire society feels the void too: there are no models to admire and imitate, no ideal which would bring out the best, no force to counter boredom and degradation. Has the church become so weak and self-doubting that it no longer serves as a model for other hierarchies in the difficult business of ordering the existence of their members? The pope's quarrel with Michelangelo was a high moment of religious art; can the church continue producing such moments, moments when man's greatest efforts respond to divine expectation? Symmetrical to that episode was that of another pope, Paul VI, whose speech to the general assembly of the United Nations (1965) reminded the members that the church is "an expert in humanity." Nowhere did he say that the church is an expert in beauty and culture. But he did start collecting modern paintings and ordered that a special museum be built to house them. The cultural ambiance is clearly no longer the same.

It would be tempting to draw a unique line of cause and effect between such episodes (those of which the two popes were protagonists), in order to argue that the state of culture depends on the coming together of favorable circumstances, on a certain social structure such as a hierarchically ordered society, or on the rise of a new class. To be sure, the last thousand years in the West owe much to the combination of a stable order and social mobility, and to the resulting steady flow and exchange of ideas and forms in the public square: universities, law faculties, art schools, princely courts, academies, publishers. The institution of the church has been perhaps the main participant, most often the directing one, in these exchanges. Yet even at the height of its power, in the twelfth to the fourteenth centuries, the authority of the church "was exercised, for example over universities, 'its own creations, less as the source of prescribed doctrine than as a general intellectual framework, the supplier of a wealth of scholarly concepts." "To philosophize," wrote the rather unorthodox Siger of Brabant (whom Dante places next to Thomas Aquinas in the *Paradise* in spite of, or because of, their head-on clashes), "is to search for more than the truth, for what other philosophers said."[8] It is difficult to imagine a more important task in the formation of culture.

This task the church cannot relinquish, as it cannot relinquish the missionary task. It is called upon to exercise it in the coming centuries in many parts of the world where "modernization" is generally equated with a takeover of traditional societies by Western industry and technology. The task is equally delicate in the West and in the rest of the world, on account of the ideological or religious blocs that oppose any active role by the church. It is of course not for Rome to replace the dominant religions and cultural ambiance, but Rome must be a visible presence. In the West, this is feasible. The prevailing ideologies are to a large extent formed from expropriated Christian concepts regrouped, reinterpreted, and systematized around opposite objectives. Catholic thought has therefore remained recognizable everywhere in the West, and the language carrying its message is intelligible in spite of the mostly hostile reception by representatives of modernity. In the non-Western world the task is harder, but there the local religions and philosophies are also less hostile. They are too ossified either to cooperate wisely with the modern trends or to offer alternatives. Thanks to its experience with all races and systems of belief, the church is capable of offering mediation. It is a two-way affair. The church brings its experience and knowledge (from now on also its local clergy) at a crucial time of modernization; the third world, in need of a bridge not traveled

8. *Philosophes médievaux des XIIIe et XIVe siècles* (Bibliothèque médiévale, 1986), p. 38. In contrast, let us quote an opposing statement by St. Thomas, a contemporary of Siger: "The study of philosophy is not destined to inform us of what other people thought, but of what truth is" *(In libros de caelo et mundo exposito)*, p. 75.

by eager material ambitions, offers the church a sensibility still receptive to the cult and to the sacred. Perhaps the church's benefit would be greater than its gift: the road to its new universality necessarily bypasses the blocked avenues of the West. It opens through immersion in the non-Western world where hopes and half-dormant energies are becoming visible. This may be the condition for the church to rediscover its universal vocation.

Generally then, the presence of the *cult* in culture is the condition needed for the rise and survival of culture. Two observations on the matter. First, since culture is an ensemble of words, attitudes, tastes, achievements, and aspirations it cannot be organized and planned, and, while it usually finds institutional channels, it is not an institution. Its coming into existence is not decided by individuals or groups. It does not respond to needs; its course and phases are neither predetermined nor predictable. If anything can be said about "culture" outside its origin in and crystallization around the cult, it is that it is an interaction of innumerable acts and thoughts, over a long time and a vast territory. Of all human endeavors, only cult—that is, religious belief—can sustain such a network of conscious and directed acts and semiconscious, quasi-automatic attitudes.

Such a description would, however, leave culture dissolved in an uncharacterizable mass. Therefore, the second observation suggests the existence of factors that narrow the description on the basis of a concrete evaluation of historical cultures. The cultic source indicates that culture arises, or at least becomes conscious of itself, in an elite whose social *(and cultic)* position marks it as the bearer of a model to imitate. Imitation is the strongest cement of communities; in animals it is partly replaced by instinct; in human beings it is the main social transmission belt of what one calls, for lack of a better word, values. It is generally a horizontal phenomenon, X imitating Y, but at the same time it is also a vertical one because members of society imitate those who possess admired and rare qualities or status, virtue or intelligence. At first, these imitated values are cultic values, and imitation by large numbers strengthens the cult. (Imitation, let us add, does not exclude rational and emotional consent; it is not a mere automatic adherence.) Insofar as culture is an extension and an heiress of cult, the group representing it—the cultured elite—is admired, imitated, copied. For certain schools of thought, such as the followers of Joseph de Maistre or of René Guénon, the identity of the cultic and cultural elite would be the ideal. Others repudiate both. The fact is, culture trickles down from its initial holders; it permeates social classes until its aspects, directives, and commands are internalized; they set the norms of taste, thinking, and behavior.

But the ordinary course of culture is that it proceeds by the imitation—one could also call it initiation—of great or significant achievements. Such achievements (or men, or events) create around themselves concentric circles, areas of impression, which then connect and interact with the waves of other circles, similarly created, by others. Raw talent, genius, and aspiration exist in individuals; it is their meeting with the significant which unlocks achievement. Few are those who find significance in the daily routine and who are able to transfigure it: a leaf of grass, a whale hunt, the sunburnt tiles of Provençal roofs, the episode of David and Goliath in the Bible. The achievement will be Melville's, Cézanne's, Michelangelo's. Others need objects already focussed: the education of heroic youth as found in the *Iliad;* the refined setting of Versailles under King Louis XIV; the cacophony of Manhattan. The strands of creation and imitation are as endless as ripples on the ocean. But for the end product to be culture, the education of taste sets the norm. Contemporaries, and then posterity, will tell what attracts and inspires—the great poets of the Augustan Age or the circus gladiators in Nero's.

It is not our business here to trace the usual course of culture to its high point, then to its decline. The fact that cultures follow one another, however, suggests three observations: they decay when the cultic core is no longer animated and believed in by those supposed to uphold it; the cult is replaced, in the same culture area or elsewhere, by other cults;

and the new cult inspires in due time a new culture and a new elite. The period between cultures is always rough; raw instincts dominate even those who prepare, often unknown to themselves, the next ascent.

The Catholic church alone is in a position to take up the cause of creating a new culture because it alone in the West has kept the cult alive even among doubts, tribulations, and cultural ruin. This kind of "spiritual imperialism," carried out together with spiritual centers elsewhere, has remained the world's hope, over against insipid planetary renewal movements, peace initiatives, and ecumenical brotherhoods. It remains the genuine desire of millions who want to climb out of cultural misery and spiritual void. The matter appears unrealistic now because we have become accustomed to adore the modern idols, mainly technology and economism. We do not imagine that anything can be realized outside the channels cut by these two, in combination, in the world of possibilities. Yet history is witness that great things are accomplished outside, most often against, the routine-sanctioned framework.[9] The church is infinitely resourceful because it possesses the story that is always new, that of Christianity and beyond, the summed-up essence of mankind's spiritual experience. Many men and women at one point in their lives stop, reflect, and, as it were, turn around. The Greeks called it *metanoia*, Chris-

---

9. We are now accustomed to believe that the course of events is generally dictated by great historical forces, studied by macro-sociology, macro-economics, statistical thinking in blocks, etc. The role of the individual and of the intangible is minimized. But take a look at another picture. The first dent that Marxism suffered was not the consequence of penury in the Soviet Union and the rise of national minorities, but Solzhenitsyn's arrival in the West (1974); the first halt to Western sexual aberration was not signalled by any presidential committee report from Washington, but by the encyclical *Humanae Vitae* (1968); the post-1945 world did not evolve, as the experts predicted, according to Orwell's pattern of a planet codominated by the superpowers, but toward a politically multiform world which lives again as it always lived: with conflicts, regional wars followed by pacts that get broken, religious revivals and regional cooperation, mass migrations and a worldwide trend to create national homelands, etc. In other words, history as usual. The point is that mankind is the nesting place of enough freedom to produce constantly the incalculable, and that these incalculables account for more originality than what committees of planners can bring forth.

tians call it conversion, others call it illumination, maturation, wisdom, or mystical encounter with the Godhead. It transforms the life of the person who experiences it. The seemingly strange thing is that it transforms lives following the same path, even though the point of irruption, the initial spark, differs widely from one to the other. The original motive may be discontent or joy, the discovery of the world's falsehoods or of the beauty which fills the world. Once the discoveries are made, the paths converge: there is the exhilaration that life has value; the intellectual satisfaction that words have meaning; the sudden comprehension that one has climbed a wall and that those remaining on the other side, while in spiritual misery, should not be despised but helped over; the grasp of history and time as not empty or irrelevant but posting guidelines and insights for human nature; finally, the supernatural perception that all these strings are pulled together by a being who can only be called God. Life will be lived and choices made after reaching this point, but both in a purer light, with one's feet on more solid ground. There is never a terminus, but always the gladness of arrivals.

In counting the steps of this sudden, yet at the same time gradual, comprehension, the astonishing thing is not the individual turning-around but rather the similarity of the steps. It is as if a structure were at work, a guideline for all the impatiences, an indication that the steps are yours but that others take them too.

What we find here is the path of religion, but also of culture as we spoke about it and about them together. They do not move on the same plane, yet they form one network. Religion gives meaning to culture and keeps it alive by reinforcing acts of culture from its own sources. No cultural epoch would display the unity of its works—which allows a marvellous diversity—without faith in the transcendent reality permeating it. Gothic churches, but also "pagan" Renaissance sculpture and painting; Bach's, Handel's, Vivaldi's, and Mozart's compositions, but also nineteenth-century sensuous impressionists—all were parts of a cultural inspiration because they all inherited standards from religion: reference to

something beyond the senses that we must nevertheless cap-
ture—love of form, the marveling attitude before nature, the
human body, the world of colors, sounds, and shapes. The
present emptiness of art, the wish to distort, to forget, indicates
the fury felt on finding nothing behind events, objects, and
humankind. When representatives of modern culture speak of
the Christian religion, the standard label they give it (and this
is a favorable view!) is that it is a legend; they call it "the
Christian mythology." Stories in Hellas about Zeus, Apollo,
and Aphrodite were often cruel or libidinous stories, but
nobody imagined them to be real, and the philosophers,
whether Plato or Epicurus, soon reduced these deities to mere
mythological figures. But with the vanishing of even mythological god figures, Greek art and literature no longer produced
masterpieces or heroic tales, and Greek forms of life no longer
elicited admiration. Posterity called it decadence. In the last
analysis, Western culture depends on whether the Christian
story as told by the church is a true and believed story.

This chapter is about *culture* only in the sense that the *church*
has always been a determinant element in its origin, formation,
and guidance. So has the state, and for the same reason both
state and church used to construct the political-moral edifice
of society. The modern controversy in this respect, somewhat
under the surface of agreement and compromise, is whether
civil society is able to shoulder the earlier, culture-creating
function of state and church, and able to define and lay the
groundwork of a new culture, profane and desacralized. This
would be a "humanist" culture, free of state power and without
the religious sacred—in other words a secular culture, the first
in history.

This endless controversy has in fact been settled: civil
society has not created any kind of culture—it lives off the past,
at times constructing a new framework, at other times mutilat-
ing that which exists—but it uses the prestigious label still
attached to the word *culture*. It puts this label on any merchandise upon which its momentary appetite sets its gaze. Thus we
have the proletarian culture, feminist culture, youth culture,

liberated culture, each of them ambitious to win the fleeting day for itself, to impose itself as the fashion and profit by the novelty. In contrast to the maturation and discernment of all former cultures, modern culture wants everything and wants it quickly. The state of affairs which arises from these claims and demands are for all to see—for those, that is, who do not participate in the rush of fashions, the concocted formulas with curious customers in view, the absentminded stare at the random combinations and the immediately profitable.

The new element in the hasty assemblages of contemporary culture is the drastically diminished participation of state and church. The first is present in the process but merely as a meek registering agency of ad hoc tastes and a disburser of funds to the first comer or to the most insistent lobby. It is pathetic, with the Periclean, Augustan, or Medici state in our memory, to watch the government at the federal or municipal level accept with an eager me-tooism the financial burden of whatever happens to strike the fancy of the organizers of this or that "cultural event." This conforms to the state's actual loss of power and prestige, its loss of taste and competence, and the consequent dilettantism in matters belonging to culture. Civil society, the real formulator of today's culture, possesses the monopoly on the public discourse and thus on taste.

The part that the church is playing in the formulation of contemporary culture is even more pathetic and minimal, since it has ceased to be a patron of art (replaced by what is called the "social concern") and a provider of funds. The church's cultural representatives, if the term has any relevance at all, are driven by bad conscience and by the resulting bad taste; they have withdrawn from all participation in culture. Their presence in that area, once enormous and beneficial, is signalled by a kind of morbid insistence that the urban and rural landscape, both marked traditionally by religion—the church steeple, the monastery, and the cathedral (village, wilderness, town) should become religiously undifferentiated. The consequence of this self-effacement is the dreary ecclesiastico-industrial style. The church-sponsored buildings which throughout history were shapers of taste have become nondescript landmarks of the wasteland, neutral structures which hardly dare announce their destination and not at all their glory.

More than fifty years ago, T. S. Eliot wrote the following lines: "[Is] the universal church today . . . more definitely set against the World than at any time since pagan Rome? I do not mean that our times are particularly corrupt; all times are corrupt. I mean that Christianity, in spite of certain local appearances, is not, and cannot be, within measurable time, 'official.' The World is trying to experiment with attempting to form a civilized but non-Christian mentality. The experiment will fail; but we must be very patient in awaiting its collapse; meanwhile redeeming the time: so that the Faith may be preserved alive through the dark ages before us; to renew and rebuild civilization, and save the World from suicide."

Let us draw our conclusion from these words, as if they were from a kind of cultural scripture and we wished to interpret them as the text for today. "Official Christianity," as Eliot calls it, has always been only part of the church's life, but even this part is now regarded by civil society as an impertinent interference. While it is neither unjustified nor an interference—Aristotle rightly brought together ethics and politics, and ethics *is* the church's concern—the repeated humiliations and losses of form and substance that Christianity has suffered at the hands of the unofficial religion of civil society (secular humanism) certainly justify the church's withdrawal from "politics" when that will occur. This is what was argued in this and the preceding chapters, trying to suggest the two other fields of activity for the church to focus on: the renewal of the missionary task and the shaping of culture. Eliot speaks of "redeeming the time so that Faith may be preserved alive through the dark ages before us; to renew and rebuild civilization and save the World from suicide." It could not be phrased with a deeper Christian wisdom.

Epilogue

There are those who argue that the factors and dynamics behind the weakening of Catholic presence, influence, and teaching in the last fifty years are not obvious; and they deny that any weakening has occurred. According to them, the church has instead been freed of a number of historical burdens and limiting traditions, such as those emanating from the state and even from the church's own weight as a top-heavy, hierarchical, and legalistic disciplinarian institution. And it is true that the state used to have a say, often a decisive say, in certain matters such as the nomination of bishops and, indirectly, the election of popes. It is also true that the concordats signed by the church with various states in the course of the nineteenth and twentieth centuries were compromises drawing the line of reciprocal interference. It is fitting to add here, however, that the state yielded just as often; some of the outstanding cases are the conflict between St. Ambrose of Milan and Emperor Theodosius, between Pope Gregory VII and Henry II, between Pius XI and Mussolini's Italy, and dozens if not hundreds of other cases where the church imposed its viewpoint on the state. No institution working among man has ever been without serious limitations. Responsibilities are mutual and shared; compromises are frequent.

The argument of this book is that the separation from the state by no means "liberated" the church from its servitudes; it only shifted—and aggravated—them under the aegis of civil society, a definitely harsher master than the state. In less than

173

a century, civil society has not only neutralized and marginalized the Christian religion, but has also replaced it with a godless and immoral ideology that has become—unstated and unwritten, but all-pervasively—the real and effective creed of most regimes in the West. Those who say that liberal civil society is essentially pluralistic and therefore a guarantor of an institutional and confessional freedom to the church, refuse to grasp the nature of the mechanism through which a "soft ideology" like liberalism penetrates minds and attitudes. It is a flatterer of egos and appetites.

As we have indicated, this "soft ideology" and its variants have a well-established name: *liberalism*. A radically individualistic philosophy, liberalism turns every man into a sovereign over himself, thereby cutting the natural ties of existence. True, liberal theory pretends that these isolated and self-ruled individuals have entered a primordial contract as the basis and justification for co-existence. However, this contract works with a goal of secured individual rights and desires, not any sense of corporate belonging or responsibility. In the event that individuals are not satisfied in this contract, they may secede and become members of another one.[1]

With emphasis on the *self* and his *rights*, the common and enduring denominators of existence—things like truth, the moral good, and the political *bonum commune*—have been steadily relativized and whittled down. The result is a social and ideological free-for-all and hedonism. As a consequence, not only does liberalism reduce the church to a pressure group, but the supposed freedom it grants her in the public place is countered by the much greater freedom that nihilistic and hedonistic ideologies enjoy. Since according to the rules of the

---

1. This is now also happening in the church where the liberal pattern gains ground. Rebellions and moral secessions are daily occurrences, further weakening and ridiculing an already fragile authority. "Can a woman be saved by a male savior?" asks a feminist graduate of the Claremont School of Theology. Another Sister says that by taking on a male body, Jesus assumed the sin of "belonging to the oppressor class." These are grotesque illustrations of an essential secession, aggravated by the fact that their authors "secede inside," claiming to represent the true church over against Rome.

game all pressure groups are equal, the church as merely one of them is forbidden to raise her voice against rampant immorality and aberration; by doing so she would break the social contract, the only sacred thing in modern civil society. The ambition to put an immanentist religion in the place of transcendental religion—the cult of man instead of the veneration of God—was implicit in liberalism from the beginning.

All the weaknesses that the church displays in today's world—from the overanxious ecumenistic pleas of Vatican II to the absurd, vulgar, and timeserving behavior of bishops, theologians, and clergy—are derived from the adoption by the contemporary church of liberal modes of thought, chief among which is the belief that mankind has reached maturity and can now sacralize itself as its ultimate and exalted product. Whether "liberal" or "socialist," the world is now adored for itself and its self-emancipation from eternally binding moral truth. Having appointed itself the embodiment of the Absolute (the consequent degrading of Jesus Christ finds its explanation here), the world sets up a counter-church. Concretely, this church consists of those ecclesiastics and laymen who, in their anti-Roman rage and contempt, or out of mere opportunism, seek shelter among the newly powerful: the media, the mega-universities, and ideological pressure groups. Their objective is to dismantle the church. Thus civil society does not directly interfere with the affairs of the church; it entrusts this task to its secularist pressure groups.

Now it is natural that many Catholics, caught between the attractions of the modern world (peace with liberal society, accommodation with its ideology, espousal of its spirit, suspicion that the church will end up by yielding to pressure and temptation) and an uncompromising orthodoxy, resort to (a) analyzing the present situation—as we are doing here— and (b) concluding that the best course of action is the acceptance of the liberal world and its irresistible imperatives. The trouble with this position is that it accepts history according to the liberal vision, as one-dimensional and immanent—as if some inherent principle inside history worked itself out, like the universal spirit of Hegel's philosophy or the universal materiality of Marx's.

Yet does history not teach us that "history" is not alone making history, that another—superior or parallel—design is also at work, call it providence, divine irruption, or *Heilsgeschichte?* Just as the existence and processes of the universe are evidently *more* than the mere unraveling of matter—namely, the action of the spirit—history must also be more than a collection of bare automatisms. It must incorporate an extra-historical spirit.

Yet to the shapers of the modern mind liberal society is the final act in history. Consequently, the supposedly correct Catholic attitude is cautious conformity to the society's injunctions, backed by its supporting evidence. The argument runs like this: We are undergoing, whether in Peking or in the Vatican, a cultural revolution oriented to the present which reduces the past to a museum piece. Peking performed its revolution by denying the validity of Confucius's teaching and by rewriting history according to Marxist lines; the Vatican performed *its* revolution at the Council which took place within its walls, and which expressly did not build on the preceding councils but affirmed its own updating on the liberal-progressivist pattern. The resulting secularization (to speak now of the Vatican only) does not mean the obliteration of the religious phenomenon; it only means that the coming civilization will not be stamped by Christianity. Instead it will be plural, planetary, without limit to freedom of expression, choice of religion, and moral option.

The church has no choice in the matter; the latest conciliar documents irreversibly push her into modernity, and she must accommodate modernity's representatives, the bearers of a new culture: radicals, inventors of new lifestyles (homosexual couples, lesbian teachers) and social norms, and abortionists. Liberalism, the cult of the world today, is for the church *aggiornamento.* Not only does the structure of liberal society—the predominance and power of pressure groups—make it impossible for the church to confront those pressure groups which advocate moral degradation; the changes within the church must mirror society's transformation along the line of secularist dogmas and attitudes. This is the tremendous significance of Vatican II: the church consented to its own secularization, surrendering to hostile ideologies in the world and in the ecclesiastical ranks.[2] The remarkable thing for Catholics in this new agenda is that they are addressed as if they were independent of, and practically outside, the church, their magisterial and institutional framework.

Possibly the most generous formulation of the coming alliance of culture and the sacred is announced by Polish philosopher Leszek Kolakowski, among others. Secularization, he wrote in 1973, is gradually accomplished before our eyes, but it does not come as the denial of the sacred, but rather as the abolition of any differences between the sacred and the profane. The consequence is that Christianity gives up insistence on evil (presumably original sin) and adopts the Teilhardian view that evil had been attached to evolution's early brutishness and materiality, which now have given way to belief in universal salvation and to an all-pervasive spirituality. After all, Kolakowski argues, the purely profane world as such would not be viable—it does not exist, because whatever men think and do is "affected by an added significance" for which mere empirical observation cannot account. This added significance confers a value on all phenomena, providing a structure, a cultural meaning, to a collection of brute facts.

True, Kolakowski warns of the danger that, in its self-satisfaction and arrogance, the profane world may dismiss the sacred addition, in which case the structureless phenomena of society, and society itself, would collapse with their illusions. The Polish thinker—whose long journey from Marxist materi-

2. It may be countered that under John Paul's pontificate Rome has removed Frs. Küng and Curran from representing church teaching at universities; that the pope has begun appointing orthodox bishops; that the Vatican imposed a period of silence on some ultraradical priests and theologians like Frs. Schillebeeckx and Boff. Yet all these moves are quasi-secret and show timidity rather than fully and openly exercised authority. Heterodoxy, in spite of sporadic Roman reaction, is rampant; it is like a guerrilla force, attacking at unexpected times and places, multiplying the skirmishes against a slow-moving and dwindling army, unsure of itself and its good right.

alism should be acknowledged—believes that the profane is not autonomous and cannot afford to carve out a nonspiritual course for itself. We note, however, that even this friendly witness (*a*) reduces the religious to the cultural, and (*b*) prepares a "reasonable" Christianity, as some Renaissance reformists and Erasmians and the Enlightenment thinkers Lessing and Kant tried to do before him. Since then only the style of the attacks has changed. In short, Christian entry into the modern world involves a vast compromise: the *profane*, recognized by the most generous as imperfect by itself, signs a new kind of concordat with the *spiritual*. Their offspring is expected to be the New Culture.[3]

Our own analysis of the contemporary situation and its causes is more prudent than that of any of the accommodationists, taking into account the many-layered potentials of history without dismissing the recurrence of historical patterns. True, the description of accommodationist systematizers is at times factually correct. But should we also agree that these facts and events are products of a unilinear evolution, and thus irreversible, sociologically and scientifically determined, and unchangeable? Should we also add that *therefore* they are desirable and good? Is it not more prudent and reasonable to suggest, as we did throughout these chapters, that the recent great changes in the church's position are not the consequences of actions by the Holy Spirit, but rather consequences of the rise of ideologies—chief among them liberalism—and of civil society?

In this way, nobody can argue that liberalism is the last change, that ours is the final society, that today is the last word

3. What is forgotten in this thesis, advocated today by very powerful voices, is pointed out by Flavio Cappucci: "Once religion is deprived of its supernatural content, it will be replaced by political consciousness." The new heresies will not speak of worship, faith, or the sacraments, but rather of human solidarity, social justice, and religion as a support for class struggle. As Jaime Antunez writes in the April 1989 issue of *Crisis*, this follows the program of Italian Marxist Antonio Gramsci: the cultural infiltration of civil society, which will gradually abandon the residual religious feeling it may still possess.

in history. The door of argumentation and of coming development is left open for the promotion of new transformations,
and eventually also for a return to traditional, orthodox models.
Even a decline of liberalism can be envisaged, because this
ideology too, like others in the past, may obliterate itself
through the grim pursuit of its inherent logic—of absolute and
indiscriminate equality and desacralization. If the liberal ideologues paid attention to their own historical rise to the present
dominant position, they would admit that their ideology too is
mortal. After all, Marxist ideologues who believed that Marxism spells the end of history are now revising the once-claimed
immutability of *their* dogma. Religious fervor and orthodoxy
are just now waking them up from their slumber.

The secret conviction of Catholic accommodationists is
that the church has lost the battle against modernity. They
explain that history—and, why not, even God!—destines the
church gradually to blend with liberal society.[4] This proposition is worth its thirty silver pieces because only the blind fail
to see that the blending of church and liberal society has
prompted the mass desertion of Catholics from their religious
institutions and from the Mass. It takes an extraordinary
amount of arrogance to point at self-liquidation as progress and
renewal. Where is the inner reinforcement, the outreach, the
popularity, the warm reception by other religions that Vatican
II expected and promised? We find instead numberless gatherings of scholars who conclude, like a recent gathering in San
Francisco, that the identity of Christ is subject to question and
the gospels to suspicion; that the historical reality of Christ's
passion is an embellished fake, the promise of the Second
Coming baseless, Christ's divinity a pious invention, and the
presence of the church in history a succession of fraudulent
moves and bids for power.[5]

4. Note that while in the Marxist view historic changes are born in
violence, in the liberal view changes are gradual. The presupposition of
irreversibility and improvement is the same in both.
5. In a different but more devastating way (in view of the rank of the
signatories and their well-established shelter in the media world), German and
French theologians have attacked the pope's place as the church's supreme

If the logic of accommodationism leads to a change of such magnitude—the reappraisal of all Christianity and the church—then to be honest we ought to speak not of a renewal but of a new religion, one blending with liberal ideology and its shades of Marxism. If this is so, however, it may be advisable, even if only for reasons of methodology, to perceive in the present upheavals not the death of one religion and the rise of another, but, as this book suggests, a historically plausible reaction of Roman policy to a great, yet not insurmountable, peril. Since the main objective of the Catholic church is the preservation of the sacred deposit—faith in Christ's divinity, the integrity of doctrine and moral teaching, and the centrality of the Mass—the manner of protecting and transmitting it to future generations involves a temporary partnership with powerful outside forces without yielding an iota on doctrine. For more than a century, the "outside forces" have been liberalism and its escort of militant secularists and hedonists; but liberalism nears its decline, and the church is redirecting its policies, slowly yet perceptibly, to the Left. This requires little effort since the proclivity of liberal society bends its course leftward: first democracy, then equality, socialism, cultural nihilism—things generally located in the leftist arsenal. The church follows too, politically, not doctrinally. No longer do kings, nobility, feudal or bourgeois structures and worldviews hold power, but now these powerholders do: pressure groups, street demonstrators and their organizers, the media, and the leftist-militant enclaves.

The thesis that the church is writing another chapter of her history—whether long or short no one knows—is more reasonable than the assumption of her enemies and of the enthusiastic accommodationists that a unique revolution is taking

---

teacher, his position on sexual and biomedical matters, and his freedom to appoint bishops. Since the various attacks took place in the first trimester of 1989—timed probably for the bicentennial of the French Revolution—the move may have been a concerted one. The statements ride roughshod over canon law, accepted norms and structures, and even the conciliar declarations in the spirit of which the signatories claim to have acted.

place, a new Christianity being born. The assumptions of accommodationists cannot be proven; they are the familiar fare of utopian projects. Nor is there scientific proof for our thesis that the church is changing her strategy and her partners.[6] But this thesis is at least more credible in the light of two thousand years of history.

We should by all means entertain some doubts about the success of the "leftist" turn. The church's adversaries, including her own accommodationists, are the first to advertise their belief in the "masses" whose support is, they believe, the proof par excellence that certain ideologies and popular movements are on the right track, the one on which history advances. The mass support for Marxist or democratic trends seems to them the very voice of history and of the future. In fact, those who set Vatican II and its reforms into motion used to argue that they did so in order to satisfy the mass of believers wishing to participate in a vernacular liturgy, to hear popular music, and to see other than ceremonial art in church. The statement of Paul VI relative to this idea was quoted earlier: "The good of the people demands that they may actively participate in the cult. . . . The Church sacrifices her sacred and beautiful language, Latin, . . . her tradition. . . . All this for a greater universality, reaching all" (1965).

The sacrifice and the concessions brought no fruit. We now witness how the masses desert the church and its buildings. Can one still claim that what was done served the masses and the church's universality in their midst? The masses are not found at Mass; they flock instead to three other movements which today summon their numbers and loyalty: Islam, Marxism, and the hedonism of Western culture. If Vatican II was calculated to spread the church's message wider and deeper, it

6. It is an open secret that local churches—the Chilean, the French, the German, the Dutch, and others—are subsidizing ultra-leftist, Marxist guerrilla movements out of parishioners' money. In France, the organization CFDT was taken to court by Pierre Debray and found guilty; in Chile, the Vicaria de la Solidaridad (sponsored by the local church) has been sheltering revolutionary priests; the German and Dutch churches heavily subsidize Marxist activities in South America and Africa.

was a miscalculation. After having "lost" the eighteenth and nineteenth centuries, the church has not won back the twentieth.

Yet it may have been a providential loss. What the American archbishops allegedly told John Paul at their Vatican "summit" in March 1989 has a significance beyond what they thought they said. Archbishop John May, their spokesman, informed the pope that "Americans are not accustomed to interference with their right to decide for themselves!" It seems Americans do not believe in the divine right of God just as they reject the divine right of kings. (A mayor of Chicago once said, "In America every man is king!") This is of course pure demagogy; all people submit to authority, and Americans are particularly prone to join unexamined campaigns for this or against that—on the authority, for example, of the media. But it is true that modern Western man, and not just Americans, adrift on the turbulent waters of his overrated consciousness, no longer knows up from down, his own capricious ego from legitimate authority. What Mgr. May said contains man's dismissal of God and his own self-divinization.

If this is the nature of the relationship today between Western man and God—a relationship, you remember, that was to deepen faith and bring the two closer—there remains God and non-Western man. Thus Mgr. May's words close a chapter: Western man is exhausted and spiritless; in his measureless madness he refuses the hand in which hundreds of millions rest their worries, their tortured souls, their wounded lives, and their hopes. Within that hand lies the promise of the church's third millennium.